D0144859

Models For Movers
Irish Women's Emigration to America

Ide O'Carroll

Attic Press
Dublin

© Ide O'Carroll 1990

All rights reserved. Except for brief passages quoted in newspaper, magazine, radio or television reviews, no part of this book may be reproduced in any form or by any means, electronic or mechanical, including photocopying or recording, or by any information storage and retrieval systems without prior permission from the Publishers.

First Published in Ireland in 1990 by
Attic Press
44 East Essex Street
Dublin 2

British Library Cataloguing in Publication Data
O' Carroll, Ide
    Irish women's emigration to America : models for movers.
    1. United States. Irish immigrants
    I. Title
    973.049162

    ISBN 1-85594-008-6

Grateful acknowledgement is made to Eavan Boland for permission to reprint her poem "The Emigrant Irish" first published 1983.

Leland Bardwell's poem "Exiles" is from *Wildish Things: An Anthology Of New Irish Women's Writing*, first published by Attic Press, 1989.

Cover Design: Luly Mason
Origination: Attic Press
Printing: The Guernsey Press Co Ltd

Dedication

To my Kerry Matrons, Sheila and Mary
My teacher, Professor Ruth-Ann Harris
and
My mother, Mary O'Carroll

Míle Buíochas

About the Author

Born in County Offaly, IDE O'CARROLL taught in
Bishopstown Community School in Cork for a number of years
before going to Boston in 1986. A founder member of the *Irish
Women in Boston* group, she also set up a media collective,
Trasna na dTonnta - Across the Waves, and has been a
consultant to numerous film, TV and radio documentaries on
issues relating to Ireland. She has an MA in History from
Northeastern University and is now doing doctoral work at
Harvard. She says that in order to survive while studying in the
USA she has worked at the jobs that generations of Irish women
immigrants have traditionally done - cleaning, painting, looking
after old people and waiting on tables.

Acknowledgements

Models for Movers is a condensed version of my thesis written with the direction of Professor Ruth-Ann Harris at Northeastern University in Boston. During the four years that I have worked on this project I have been welcomed into the homes of many Irish women in the United States of America. Without their willingness to share the story of their lives this work would not exist. To each and every one, especially the many who do not appear here, I offer my genuine thanks. To all at the Irish Studies Programme at Northeastern I also extend my appreciation for invaluable support at all times. John McGrath of Dedham provided a much needed link into the Gaeltacht community in Boston and John Curran of *The Sound of Erin* radio show continued to broadcast the merits of my project. Mike McCormack of the *Irish Echo* newspapers, and national director of the *Ancient Order of Hibernians* brought me in contact with Christy and Noel Halpin, Bridie's nephews, and arranged access to all of Bridie's papers. Denis Clark in Philadelphia offered encouragement at a critical stage, and provided copies of interviews he had conducted. Marie Daly of the *New England Historic and Genealogical Society* in Boston also provided me with copies of interviews with Irish immigrants.

The following institutions allowed me access to their resources and the staff were at all times helpful: Northeastern University, Harvard University, Radcliffe College - Murray Research Centre on Women, Boston College - O'Neill and Burns, Boston University, Yale University. My thanks also to the Director of Kilmainham Gaol, Patrick Long and his staff who worked hard on the Bridie Halpin section. Also, the staff at the Balch Institute for Immigration Studies at Philadelphia.

A special word of thanks to photographers Caitríona Cooke and Sandie McDade, immigrants themselves and both amateur photographers. Also, to Dearbhal Ní Chárthaigh who encouraged me from day one. Ailbhe Smyth did what fine editors do, and with the minimum upset to the author.

Throughout the four year incubation period I have personally received much love and support of all kinds. First and foremost Professor Ruth-Ann Harris, Director of Irish Studies at Northeastern who opened her library, mind, home and heart to this immigrant. Transatlantic tenderness and support came frequently and abundantly from my mother Mary O'Carroll, my sisters Maura Rea, Kay Lawler and their families. Elise Kaufman and Seamus Henchy took care of me in New York. Caitríona Cooke and Paula Herrington always helped with accommodation and work in Boston. My friend Gemma Kelleher continued to encourage from afar, as did Sheila and Mary, my Kerry matrons. In Boston, Caroline Whitbeck, Anne Rath, Maura Twomey, Teresa O'Hara, Rena Cody and na mná eile who helped me continue through the rough times. Margaret Kelleher's keen eye and probing questions mixed liberally with craic and grá were a lifeline. Finally, Katherine O'Donnell who taught me not to fear, but to believe in women's words; not to be quiet, but to speak out for myself; and to laugh and love in the face of all dragons.

Contents

Illustrations

Models for Movers
Interviews and Tapes

1920s

Nora Joyce
Bridget McLaughlin
Mary Terry Kelly

1930s

Bridgid Gilchrist

1950s

Eimear
Mary Walsh
Frances Newall Coen
Irene McKenzie
Eileen Newell

1960s

Terry Ryan Ryder

1980s

LL
RR
Leena Deevy
Teresa O'Hara
MM
BB
Fionnuala McKenna
Rena Cody
Máire Ní Bhranlaigh

Foreword

Too often history has either ignored women or included them in general accounts of the "human experience." This is particularly true of immigration history and specifically the story of Irish women immigrants to the United States of America.

In the nineteenth century three main waves of emigration from Ireland took place - before, during and after the Great Famine of the 1840s. This century has also experienced three waves where there has been a marked increase in the number of women coming to the USA - 1920s, 1950s and 1980s. In the twentieth century then, every thirty years a substantial swelling in the numbers of women emigrating has occurred. This is significant not only because it is a rise in numbers, but because some women have chosen the USA over the more convenient and possibly more short-term route to Britain.

Immigrant history is often just focused on the experience of immigrants in the host or new country. However, we need to consider the position of women in the home or old country and the reasons why they left if we are to understand the peaks in numbers from Ireland in the twentieth century. The movement may be a barometer of life at the time for women, and the position of women within the society can give insight into the migration.

The role of women in society in the periods in question must therefore be viewed in terms of its socio-economic, political and religious dimensions. In Ireland, the twenties represented a time of general conservatism with regard to women reflected later in the Constitution of 1937. Though women gained the vote relatively early, in post-Revolutionary Ireland women supported the small farm economy with the unpaid work of their bare hands. The 1950s witnessed a massive burst of emigration from an Ireland with few opportunities for paid employment in agriculture or industry, and a desire on the part of women for the higher standard of living tasted during the war years by many in

Britain. Essential to this move was a desire to distance themselves from control by family and patriarchal society.

In the past decade, the droves of women coming to the USA are rather different and seem to be seeking to escape from repressive legislation and economic hardship in Ireland. These women have been exposed to a greater level of education than the generations of Irish women who came before them. They have come through the years of the feminist movement and bring expectations of equality of opportunity from their home country to the USA. As "undocumented aliens"* they place these hopes at the doorstep of the homes within which they nanny and clean, taking up the work of their foresisters.

I believe that for Irish women, both now and in the past, the decision to emigrate reflects a conscious or unconscious decision to reject a society oppressive to women and the choice to move to a country where they know a greater level of independence and control can be exercised over their own lives. They consider the USA to be such a country.

---

* *Most "new Irish" enter the USA on visitors' visas, overstay the time allotted and become "out of status" or "undocumented" aliens.*

Introduction

The Emigrant Irish

*Like oil lamps we put them out the back:
of our houses, of our minds. We had lights
better than, newer than and then
a time came, this time and now
we need them. Their dread, makeshift example.*

*They would have thrived on our necessities.
What they survived we could not even live.
By their lights now it is time to
imagine how they stood there, what they stood with,
that their possessions may become our power.*

*Cardboard. Iron. Their hardships parcelled in them.
Patience. Fortitude. Long-suffering
in the bruise-coloured dusk of the New World.*

And all the old songs. And nothing to lose.

Eavan Boland

I have called this book *Models for Movers* because of my own desire as an immigrant woman to find and reclaim the "oil lamps," "lights," or life stories of Irish women immigrants - those beacons of bravery that have been "hidden from history", to use Sheila Rowbotham's phrase. For generations, women have been deprived of role models because of the inability or unwillingness of scholars to recognise the importance of documenting the experience of women in history. What models do, in my view, is provide the motivation for women to move in their own lives, at work, in relationships, or in some instances out of an entire society. If we know about the experiences of other women at different stages in history and in different cultures, we understand how women have coped with different situations. We can learn from these stories and apply their experience to our own lives.

By moving in some way - by making certain choices vis a vis the situation, be it as an Irish woman in 1922 deciding to emigrate - the action is a model to all to have the courage to act. This action or movement needs to be viewed in the context of different responses to power as well as in the context of oppression, resistance and liberation. "To be less powerful is not to be power-less, or even to lose all the time..."[1]

In my own experience as an immigrant to the USA what I personally found most lacking were role models and in an attempt to find them I embarked on a search of women's history. This journey has led me to consider the experiences of women of different cultures, races and class at different points in history. I travel not as a historian, but first and foremost as a woman who has questions from a feminist perspective. Hungry as I was for answers, I find the personal encounters with women to be the most fruitful and fulfilling learning ground. Following on from *Models for Movers* I have developed a multi-ethnic oral history project for the City of Boston. "Boston Listens and Learns" is an attempt by immigrant and refugee women to record and listen to one another's stories.

Ireland is especially rich in the strength of its oral tradition. Knowledge of history, culture, myth and legend is passed on verbally. To listen is to learn and to learn is to understand, and I chose to use oral histories as a main source in my work. Uncensored or not, exaggerated or faultlessly true, these accounts are valuable in many respects, not least because they are a record of what women consider to be interesting and important in their experience, and of their perception of the conditions of a particular time.

Oral history is especially important in women's history because unless they are privileged, women are often the ones with least time to sit and write; they may be illiterate but still intelligent; and they seldom value their "ordinary" lives. Theirs is primarily an oral history passed from generation to generation - or as it is expressed in Irish "ó ghlún go ghlún," literally from knee to knee.

The history of Irish women's migration to the USA is a long one dating back many centuries. However, the nineteenth century was the period of greatest movement. After the 1840s the main ethnic groups emigrating there were Jews, Italians and Irish. Irish women migrating at this time were generally unmarried. Their passage was paid for by female relatives and once established they generally assisted other women to emigrate, principally by sending home passage money. This pattern is known as female chain migration and is unique to Irish women at this time.

Models for Movers is about Irish women's continued desire and need to emigrate to the United States into the twentieth century. Although the possible reasons and explanations for this emigration of Irish women are discussed, the major focus of the book is on what women emigrants themselves have to say. Interviews with some women emigrants I spoke to are given in their entirety because, in truth, theirs is the only real picture. Our interpretation of their words is merely one path to an understanding of their life's experience. Today, with the new wave of young Irish women emigrants to the United States of America, it is timely that women of all generations have role models - models of movers, present and past.

Chapter One
Nineteenth Century Emigration
A Unique Pattern for Irish Women?

Since the 1800s in particular, Ireland has had a massive exodus as part of its heritage and this exodus continues today into the 1980s with the latest surge of emigrants to north America being referred to as the "New Irish." This drain is dramatic when reflected in relation to a population 8 million in 1841 and approximately 3.5 million (26 counties) in 1980.

In most emigration studies a clear distinction is made between push and pull factors. In nineteenth century Europe a change in the economic base from one that was primarily agricultural and rural to one that was industrial and urban created the push-pull dynamic. Some general trends in emigration to north America resulted as more hands were needed to work the industries and service the needs of expanding areas such as New England. Though Britain was obviously the first choice of many emigrating Irish, as it still is, the USA was also a most attractive pull.

The Great Famine of the 1840s and the famines which followed created the greatest push of all - imminent death. When disaster struck people died of starvation and disease or they emigrated. Financing the passage required personal funds or sponsorship. Relatives and wealthy individuals such as Vere Foster (whose women's fund sponsored 23,000 emigrants), landlords and state sources provided some sponsorship for those emigrating at this time to north America, Australia, Canada and the colonies.

However, the main source for passage money was that sent back by Irish emigrants already established in north America - about 34 million pounds in remittances between 1848-1887, two fifths of which came as pre-paid passage. This is typical of the pattern of "chain migration" particularly strong amongst women and is a wonderful testament to those who had gone ahead. The social and economic change that raged through the country in post-Famine Ireland resulted in two significant factors which themselves acted as catalysts and greatly affected the life chances of women. One was an end to small landholdings in favour of larger ones, while the other was a near moratorium on marriage. Only one family member would now inherit the farm, usually the eldest boy. The options for Irish women were limited to an arranged marriage, unpaid work on the family farm, or emigration. This increasingly patriarchal situation left little or no choice for women.

The majority of emigrants from Ireland after 1820 were unmarried. Also, although pre-Famine movement from Ireland to the USA was largely balanced between the sexes, the post-Famine trend saw a steady increase in the number of women until they actually outnumbered men in the period 1881-1900. This pattern differed greatly from the movement of Jews or Italians at this time. Jews tended to travel in family groups and Italian men came alone sometimes arranging to bring family later.

Many Irish women emigrants supported families in Ireland and paid for the passage of female relatives. The Great Famine experience had taught them that Irish families with large numbers could not sustain themselves. In America, the most common choice of work for these women was domestic service and to a lesser extent work in textile factories. Domestic service guaranteed income, accommodation and a greater level of autonomy than at home. This may be interpreted as an astute move in relation to market demand and also a rejection of traditional family life and its inherent male power structure. This choice differed greatly from their Italian and Jewish counterparts whose work was carefully monitored, and selected by men. Therefore Irish women did not react to economic opportunity in terms of traditional cultural values. Indeed, by their actions they contradicted the idea of women as dependant by forming female networks for others to emigrate, ensuring a niche for themselves within the marketplace and in general directing their lives independently, free from family constraints. Born out of a time of crisis, women's migration in the late nineteenth century provided a network and a lifeline to a relative freedom. The road had been broken by those models who had the courage and tenacity to strike out for themselves. Other Irish women would follow this proud legacy all through the twentieth century.

By 1921 a total of 8 million people had emigrated since 1801. This represented the total population of Ireland before the Famine. The post-Independence movement was again from the rural areas of Ireland and consisted of the "young and most active" (Drudy). Independence had not stopped the haemorrhage of people. Civil war, world recession, trade barriers and the First World War crippled the country and hindered industrial development. The numbers in agriculture declined and people were forced to look for employment elsewhere.

From the start of the twentieth century, through post-Independence Ireland and up to the 1950s, a preponderance of women emigrated from Ireland. This mirrors the pattern established in the late nineteenth century, though much of this twentieth century movement, especially in the 1950s, was to Britain.

This important swing in the destination pattern occurred after the 1920s when Britain became the destination of choice. Important to this swing were the USA Quota Acts of 1921 and 1924. With the 1921 Act, a numerical ceiling was placed for the first time on those entering the USA. Having to deal with the USA consul in Ireland was an added difficulty and the quotas went unfilled. As well as this, the economic depression in the USA during the 1930s greatly reduced the availability of work. Irish emigration to the USA slowed to a trickle of approximately seven thousand a year in the 1950s from a previous high of over twenty four thousand a year in the 1920s.

The pattern of emigration from post-Independence Ireland points clearly to a shift from the USA to Britain, to increasing restrictions on those choosing the USA and to the predominance of women among those who emigrated. The women who chose the USA as their destination this century did so knowing it to be the more difficult, less travelled of the two routes.

Nora Joyce's sister and family, Inis Meán

Nora Joyce's sister's child, Inis Meán, c. 1914

Chapter Two
Ireland in the 1920s
Far from Roaring!

To be a woman in Ireland in the 1920s was not easy. Though the society to which they belonged was in a state of dramatic political upheaval in the early part of the decade, they were needed in this political/revolutionary process only for as long as it took to establish a new - and partitioned - Ireland.

Women were spoken to directly in the Proclamation of 1916 and their country was addressed in womanly terms:

> Irishmen and Irishwomen: In the name of God and of the dead generations from which she receives her old tradition of nationhood, Ireland, through us summons her children to her flag and strikes for her freedom.
> *Poblacht na hEireann*: The Provisional Government of the Irish Republic

Earlier, such rhetoric might have wooed women into giving their lives in the nationalist struggle, but as soon as the Irish Free State was established in 1922 the honeymoon was over. As women in revolutions the world over know, liberation of the people does not always mean women's liberation. Although not an absolute settlement of Irish affairs, as the partition of Ireland testified, the Treaty offered for the first time in centuries a measure of self-determination for 26 of Ireland's 32 counties. However paltry, it was an opportunity for Ireland to outline its position with regard to women.

Why was it then that, as the Irish Free State began to define itself - an Ireland of twenty six counties, beginning to be freed from imperialism - women were sent a very definite message of subservience to a rural, conservative male Eire? Was this message so powerful as to send women fleeing the country?

The answer to this question lies in the link between the maintenance of a primarily agricultural economy as an ideal for the new Irish Free State and the need for a large pool of unpaid female labour as a basis for such an economy. What was in essence a distinct hesitation on the part of the political leadership to modernise, a desire to maintain a country of small farms, and the continuance of the Sinn Fein ideal of self-sufficiency could only be achieved if women were "kept in their place." The catholic church contributed to this patriarchal oppression of women by its willingness to reinforce the image of subservient womanhood as the ideal for catholic Irish women, in a country where the majority of the population was catholic.

Farmers were reluctant to subdivide land or to hand over the family farms and therefore people married later and there were fewer marriages. Since tradition had it that the eldest son would then be the sole inheritor of the family farm, women in rural areas could only remain at home, working as an unpaid member of the extended family. The scenario of the spinster woman (a position of much ridicule and scorn) was very much alive. Should she marry (and the choice was not hers), the woman would need some bargaining power in the form of a dowry to make her more attractive in terms of an investment for the family into which she would marry. The pattern of late marriage was the primary factor which was, to quote social scientist Robert E Kennedy, "the essential social institution which motivated and permitted individuals to remain permanently single, or to marry at a relatively late age". Late marriages contributed to Ireland's unique demographic trend with a significant decrease in population from 1841 to 1961. As Nora Joyce (born 1910) of the Aran Islands recalls:

> Arranged marriages, of course there was. They all made matches then. There was no boys and girls going together.

The avenues to acquiring an independent source of income were not there and families were hard pressed to raise large numbers of children in times of great hardship, making dowries something rare indeed. Farmwork was not easy and its hours were unending. The economic reality for Irishwomen in the 26 counties especially, was that the work they did, the products they processed, or the animals they cared for were owned by a male, be he father, brother, or husband. Whether churning to make butter or spinning to create cloth, the means of production were owned by a male, who was under no obligation to reward this effort with payment. Again, Nora Joyce comments:

> There was work all the time ... we worked in the fields before we went to school, and when we came home every evening. Sheep and cattle, chickens and banabhs and sows breeding them ... boiling potatoes, planting and digging and hauling them in ... We went through all that. Cut our own turf too. Before you were able to go out to the fields to work you were ... doing all the odds and ends around the house.

For young or old work never ended.

> They didn't want you not to be busy.

Indeed, a woman could be busy with the hard physical work around the farm but when it came to finance the opinion of woman's judgement with regard to matters monetary was such that she was not allowed to sell animals at fairs, although she was sometimes allowed to sell eggs and butter.

As woman of the house she was expected to keep a fire going constantly, bake bread, prepare meals, wash and mend clothes, draw water, clean the house, feed and milk cows, make butter, raise fowl, bear and raise children, help at harvest time with hay and turf: "My mother seemed to be pregnant all the time ... there was nobody sitting around to be babied, and there was a baby every fifteen months" (Margaret Carlson - 1920s emigrant). Her return for such effort was to be venerated as the "Irish mother", a true martyr, given the abuse she had to take. "My mother said she was pregnant twenty years of her life, she forgot exactly when I was born." (Winifred Geary - 1920s emigrant). For many women even the respect given a "martyr" was not available to them since they remained single. The martyred mother was an ideal of womanhood propagated by the Irish male politicians of the 1920s, especially later in the decade by the powerful de Valera (whose own mother remained in Brooklyn during much of his childhood). Their picture was of a suffering but saintly woman content with her lot, a Christian willing to accept her lot as the will of God. Small thanks for such agricultural slavery in this patriarchal prison. This image is somewhat akin to the concept of *marianismo* more popular in Latin American countries, and similarly effective as a means of social control by patriarchy.

The options other than marriage were to go and work in the towns or to emigrate. As 'indentured' servants, women went to work in grocery stores and clothing departments in the towns or as domestic servants, with the hope of some level of liberation through marriage.

In the shops and large houses the employers were males, the division of labour was strictly defined and the disparity in wages reflected the continuance of women in the subservient role. What the shopkeepers had done was simply to mirror the attitudes prevalent toward women in rural areas, a fact that emphasises the national dimension of women's subordination and oppression.

Was this the entire picture for all Irish women? Was it merely a *fait accompli*? Indeed no. Three significant parts of the picture still have to be taken into account:

* those women who did become directly involved in the politics of the time through revolutionary groups and political parties
* the situation for women living in the more urban areas of Ireland and
* the unique situation of Irish women in northern Ireland.

Women In The National Struggle

Lest it be forgotten, women were a vital element in the 1916 Rising and the New Sinn Fein of 1917 attracted many of those women who had sought a more militant role in the revolution. Women had fought hard and won the right to vote. In the early decades of the twentieth century in Ireland revolutionary and suffrage movements had been the order of the day, both of them were open to the collective action of women, though sometimes only on the terms of the male leadership. Significant women leaders did emerge in both movements. Hanna Sheehy-Skeffington and Constance Markievicz being but two examples. However, both Hanna Sheehy-Skeffington and Countess Constance Markievicz became more involved with their nationalism than their feminism as their political influence increased.[2]

Both of these women were models of the leadership which elite educated Irish women were capable of showing at this time in Ireland. Hanna, an eloquent orator and public speaker, was imprisoned and went on hunger strike several times as a result of her militant action for the cause of suffrage. A founder of the Irish Women's Franchise League, Hanna and her husband Francis, also committed to feminist ideals, worked together on a number of publications. The *Irish Citizen* for example was a voice for Irish feminism, pacifism, nationalism and socialism. The demise of the publication in September 1920 marks the point at which Hanna totally dedicated herself to the nationalist cause "the national struggle overshadows all else." (Hanna Sheehy-Skeffington).[3]

Interestingly, women were accorded little public recognition of their role in the 1916 Rising. The image of rebel and patriot was male, and not one Irishwoman signed the 1916 proclamation. Patriot songs venerated the men of the struggle - Kevin Barry, for example - and women were noticeably absent. Constance Markievicz is an exception to the general pattern of the recognition of women in Irish politics. Of the six women deputies elected to the British Parliament in the election of 1923, Margaret Pearse, Kathleen Clark, Mary McSwiney, Kate O'Callaghan, Dr Ada English and Constance Markievicz, only Constance Markievicz was not related in some way to a male who had died in the earlier 1916 Rising and only she would serve more than one term. It seemed that Involvement in Parliamentary politics was therefore male defined, and dependent, for women, on their relationship to a male, an accurate reflection of the position of women nationwide in all spheres of life. This perception serves to obscure the individual contribution of women. Of the thousands of ordinary/extraordinary women who fought for the nationalist cause, few were rewarded for their effort and no story exemplifies this point more than that of Bridie Halpin which follows later in this Chapter.

Women in the Cities

Ireland in the 1920s was in a "state of chassis." (O'Casey). There was acute economic instability, with unemployment running at 130,000[4]. The depression of the 1920s compounded the problems of a newly elected conservative Free State government under Cosgrave and the 26 counties experienced chaos in economic terms as agricultural prices dropped in the middle of the decade and exports also suffered. The Free State government could do little to care for its most needy citizens since it was striving to keep expenditure down and not tax the population further. The consequence was acute need, especially in the cities. A strike of port workers which lasted six months in 1923, and the poor weather of 1923/24 which affected agricultural workers, were surely times of particular concern for women whose primary responsibility was the care of the family. The many social problems especially evident in the cities could not be attended to by a government with tight purse strings.

The administration under Cosgrave was made up of large numbers of the prosperous middle classes and large farmers (the main body of support for his party, Cumann na Gaedheal) who were not overly sympathetic to the call for assistance from urban dwellers.

Women in Northern Ireland

The general picture in northern Ireland (the six counties partitioned under the Treaty) is quite distinctive where women are concerned since there was greater industrialisation and a history of women employed in waged work outside the home. Whether the opportunity offered by industry to work for wages liberated women or not is a matter of debate. Some would argue that the double burden of waged organised work stripped the women of a certain degree of autonomy with regard to work pace, content and location and women were in fact still burdened with the responsibility for childcare and domestic work. Indeed, this double burden continues in most cultures where women are perceived as being "liberated."

The experience of the majority of women in northern Ireland in the 1920s is best understood by viewing the lives of two women and listening to their descriptions of living conditions and work experience at that time. Both women chosen are protestants because in most cases catholics migrated into industry in the north relatively late, and then of course, found themselves shut out.

Betty Sinclair, born 3 December 1910 to a protestant working class family in Hooker Street, part of the Ardoyne district of

north Belfast, recalls: "Our standard of living was pretty low."
When Betty was born, her mother, aged 29 and a textile worker,
was back at the mill within 10 days of the birth. "They only took
off the absolute minimum time from the mill. There was a legend
I only learned afterwards that the only time the women ever had
any rest was when they were having their children. When we
were very young she went to work around six o'clock in the
morning until six in the evening." In 1925 at the age of fifteen,
taken into the mill by her mother to be taught the trade of
reeling, Betty Sinclair found the work hard and constant:
"During the 1920s the conditions of the working class were
severe. The industrial base of west Belfast was the Linen
Industry and the largest mill was owned by the Ewarts ... The
rates for piece-work [were] constantly manipulated to reduce
earnings." Reelers made their money by piece-work only and
were therefore under constant pressure to maintain a steady pace
of work. "When you were working on piece-work some of the
women would hardly take time to take their mid-day meal. They
would be in early in the morning, turning the reel by hand, you
know, before the power came on. But I always refused to do that.
In fact my mother got very worried because I was ready to stop
in the evenings ten minutes before stopping time, and mother
said, "They'll pay you off". Some of the reelers would make slip
knots and then, when the yarn went to the winders, they were in
trouble. Instead of the yarn flowing it would break. I never
learned how to make a slip knot because mother taught us, and
she taught [us] very well. She was a good worker, a quiet
worker, so sister and I learned properly."

Coming from a home of trade unionists Betty quickly got
interested in politics especially during the 1929 elections and
later became one of the leading members of the Communist
Party of Ireland.

Sadie Patterson was also born into a working class protestant
family, in 1906, in the Shankill area of Belfast. She started work
at twelve years of age when her mother died, leaving her to tend
to her six brothers and sisters. In the linen mills she helped
organise the women textile workers and later became the first
woman official of the Transport and General Workers Union of
which she said "If the men in the movement pass more pubs and
fewer resolutions we'd be a good deal better off." Describing life
in the mills she said of women: "We were plentiful and cheap.

The working week was 55 hours and many a time we worked 60; and no overtime was paid. A holiday was regarded as a lay-off without pay." Women worked until six at night. Babies were born and women went back to work within 40 hours or they would lose their job.

> We who produced the finest linen in the world had to be content with the newspapers on our tables, too poor to buy what we produced. Often we slept on sheets made from flour bags.

Sadie rose to become one of the leaders of the women's peace movement in northern Ireland. Her life's commitment to women is expressed in the vow she made the first day of work, "I vowed that one day, somehow, they'd stop treating women as a pair of hands and recognise them for something else."

After the First World War, northern Ireland experienced a boom which declined as the 1920s progressed. In 1922, almost 25% of the insured population were unemployed and ten years later it was 27%. The decline in the market for linen would further affect the employment of women and the worsening situation of unemployment burden them further.

The tradition of northern Irish protestant women seems in the main to be one where women working outside the home were very much the norm. Their ability to contribute wages to the family income must have given them a measure of status denied most of their catholic sisters both in northern Ireland and in the twenty six counties. Their lives were nonetheless marked by the fact that they were still living under an oppressive patriarchal regime; the only difference between northern Irish women working in industry and their rural counterparts was that a stranger, and not a family member, determined the conditions of work and how the effort was rewarded. The money earned went to support the entire family and was not considered the woman's to dispose of.

The reality for women in Ireland in the 1920s was that they were to be defined in relation to their men, be they of the rural farm economy or the workers of the mills in industrial areas. When given some measure of political encouragement, women became involved to a great degree in the revolutionary struggles and the political processes of the newly emerging Ireland. However, the ideal of womanhood in the new Ireland continued to be primarily male-determined, with the rhetoric of the dead martyrs playing a major role. The acceptance of Pádraic Pearse's "poor mother" and the de Valera "comely maidens dancing at the crossroads" models for Irishwomen was complete. With the passing of Bridie Halpin we see the occluded memory of a revolutionary whose involvement was unknown even to her family. Had Bridie received proper recognition for her role, perhaps she might not have died in relative obscurity in New York in 1988.

Nothing is more blatant an example of the push back to the kitchen and the kettles as the legislation to exclude women from participation in the most rapidly expanding area of employment under the new government. The ban on married women working in the Civil Service typifies the marked irony of the re-emergence of the ideal of motherhood and enforced re-entry into domestic work. And this expansion was happening in an area traditionally considered women's work - secretarial.

The Role of the Church

The patriarchal catholic church facilitated this state of affairs in an interesting fashion. Since the numbers marrying had greatly decreased because of the experience of the Great Famine and since marriage was something that occurred much later in peoples' lives (because parents held on to the land), the ideal of chastity was elevated and sexual activity was strongly linked to sin and sinning. The result was a repression of sexual desire, bachelorhood and spinsterhood which may have contributed to the high levels of alcoholism and schizophrenia discussed by Nancy Scheper-Hughes.[5]

Priests, themselves the products of these very farm families, were well schooled in the behaviour patterns and as such were well equipped to patrol and enforce measures that would be effective enough to achieve the aims of the church in this matter. Patrick Kavanagh tellingly captures the mood and the process:

The Great Hunger

'Now go to Mass and pray and confess your sins
And you'll have all the luck', his mother said
He listened to the lie that is a woman's screen
Around a conscience when soft thighs are spread .....

> *In that country, in that metaphysical land*
> *Where flesh was a thought more spiritual than music*
> *Among the stars - out of reach of the peasant's hand*
> *Ah, but the priest was one of the people too -*
> *A farmer's son - and surely he knew*
> *The needs of a brother and sister*
> *Religion could not be a counter-irritant like a*
> *blister*

"Sex and sin. Sex and sin. No dances, no courtin', no nothin'" seemed to be the catchcries of the day. A theme that would continue well into the 1950s. Irish catholicism, so intricately enmeshed with the Republican movement, reinforced peasant patriarchal positions with regard to women.

Perhaps most important of all in any discussion of post-Independence Ireland is that the twenty six counties was homogeneous to a greater extent than it had ever been in its history, at least since the early plantations. This represented a new position of power for the catholic church. Nationalist Ireland was primarily catholic, rural, conservative and patriarchal. One can only surmise what the position for women might have been had the Boundary Commission proposal not been accepted and the 26 counties confronted with a society where women worked in factories, and where a proud protestant tradition existed, as it did in the six counties.

Out and Away
Irishwomen and Emigration in the 1920s

Given this difficult situation for women, it is not surprising that large numbers of Irish women decided to emigrate to the United States, England and other countries. There had to be an attraction to make a young woman consider leaving her native home for an unknown territory. Information from reliable sources had to reassure these women that a life in London, Manchester or Boston would be in some way more liberating, interesting or lucrative than if they remained at home. Such information was constantly coming to Ireland from those who had emigrated at earlier periods and though the 1920s was a time of difficulty, women still decided to leave Ireland in search of a better way of life.

Winifred Geary, 1920s emigrant, recalls that her aunt "got the bug in me. 'You should go to America', she said. She paid my way, she did everything. She worked at Louwando's in Watertown (Boston) - a cleaning place. She was one of those ladies that never worked in a family. Usually, at that time they worked in families. But she didn't for some reason or another, she was a little different. She returned home and somebody got a husband for her and so forth...."

Winifred's aunt must have felt that the experience of emigration liberated her and her tales of America fuelled a young mind with wonderful "notions" ... "I added a lot to it ... I dreamt about it." In 1925 in Ireland Winifred felt there was also a push: "Thing is, there was nothing at home. My father and mother had enough to do to take care of the family. I didn't think of it then. When you're at that age you don't think of anyone else, you just think of yourself. Although I did have ideas that something should be done. I was very happy going."

We can therefore establish that the women who left did perceive the level of patriarchal oppression of women in the new Ireland given their clear awareness that social structures could not provide opportunities for them. For the women I talked to, the move was made mainly because there was no paying work and life on the farm held little for them. The choices women made at this time are important and the reasons for those choices, whether conscious or unconscious, are indicative of a response to a society of which they were a part but within which their lives were measured in relation to a subservience to men.

In most feminist theory and analysis the focus is on how women belong to a patriarchal system and subvert it from within. It would be difficult for women to subvert such a powerful patriarchal system as existed in Ireland in the 1920s and perhaps for many the only way to do this was to emigrate, to choose another society. Remittances from sisters, aunts, nieces or cousins who had emigrated (and were aware of the limits on women in Irish society) provided the much needed lifeline and incentive to a relative freedom.

Chapter Three
Off to America - The Outward Movement of Women in the 1920s

Throughout *Models for Movers* I have tried to remain as true and as close as possible to the oral source - the voices of the women I interviewed. In this chapter, though, there are several profiles of women who emigrated to America during tho 1920s. The five voices selected in this record represent two women whose first language was Irish, a revolutionary whose papers must speak for themselves, a Cork woman and a quiet Donegal woman. Those who speak do so in delightfully diverse accents, a factor lost in print.

Nora Joyce - Islandwoman

Nora Joyce was born on 5 April, 1910 on Inis Meán, one of the Aran Islands off the coast of Galway. The Aran Islands are part of the Gaeltacht, that portion of Ireland where Gaelic is spoken as the first language.

I n my family there was five girls and two boys. I was twelve when I finished school. Then strangers used to come for the Summer, and they'd stay in some houses for vacation. The strangers were there and one day this girl said "My mother would like somebody to help doing housework." My mother sent us off, my sister and I. I was fifteen, or like that and I didn't know what I was getting into.

Nora Joyce, Passport Photo

Nora Joyce, 1989
Photograph: Caitríona Cooke

I worked in Dundrum, Dublin for about two years, doing housework; do the wash and the cleaning. It wasn't hard work really. Delia my sister came out here. I went home (from Dublin) and then I came out after six or seven months. She came to my uncle down in Dorchester, at Andrews Square. He was a Boston policeman, Martin Connelly. The aunt took her out but she stayed with him.

I came in July and I think I was three weeks out before I went to work. Fay in Galway was the agent. My sister paid for me. I stayed in Cobh, with Mrs Sweeney's boarding house. Took us eight days to come out. The Cunard line's *Cynthia*. Left on the eighth and landed on the sixteenth (1928). My sister Delia came to Ellis island (1923). I came to Boston. On the ships you'd be sick, you know with the waves. I was travelling alone. Of course there was other people on but I didn't know anybody. There was one girl coming with me, she's dead now Lord rest her soul. She didn't pass the council (health). In six months time she tried it again and she passed.

The council was in Dublin. They stripped you, had your clothes ... do everything to you. Of course if you had TB or anything like that or sometimes if they didn't want you to work too. Sometimes the government only want a certain amount to come at certain times too. The exam was maybe a week before you'd travel.

I couldn't say a word of much English. I had some 'cause I learned it in Dublin, but if I didn't leave the island, I wouldn't even have a yes and no. It was very hard too when you go outside.

I had to go through customs. My aunt was there and Seán (Uncle?). You had to sign out if somebody was to meet you. You had your tickets and your passport and whatnot. I was home once I got here. Other children growing up, they say when asked what they want to be, say "I don't know," but since I was eight years of age I wanted to come to America. My father had an aunt who came back and later she came to live with us. I slept with her. She'd be telling us "Now if you were in America you'd be baby-sitting" or "look at the plates up on the dresser, the floors would be shining just like that." And you know when you're young.

I went to my aunt first. She used to go down the beach with the family, down the Cape in the Summer. Then they used to have an employment office in Winchester. I started for seven dollars. I went to work there and the woman said "The Irish girls come over they do more damage." They used to have a carpet sweeper then, there was no vacuums. She said they'd bang the carpet sweeper. And then she'd say "You Irish girls, you go down to church on Sunday morning and talk about jobs ... you have to do this and you have to do that." So one day I was there and I said "I'm not going to make no more muffins in the mornings unless I get a raise." "Oh", she said "You dare ask me. I'm going to call up your sister." So a couple of months after that I left that and I got a better job. She said "Can you cook?" and I said "Yes I can." "Can you make popovers?' I said "Yes I can" - and I never made a popover before in my life. I got more dollars. From seven dollars a week to twelve dollars. I was two and a half years there.

I was lonesome, then I went with this family to work. In the Fall they used to go down near Gloucester. There was a lovely section there, "Magnolia." I was upstairs and I could hear the waves coming in at night, and do you know I soaked my pillow. I loved down there because there was high rocks in one place and you could go and sit there and the broad Atlantic ... it was beautiful, it was an island. When I'd hear the waves coming in I'd start thinking they were underneath our house at home.

I used to write home. I wouldn't buy twenty five cents worth of candy bar. We'd send money home three or four times a year. In August to buy the turf for the Winter, because there was no pension. We had enough.

I met my husband when I was out here two or three years. Then they used to have showers. They used to invite the men to the shower too. It was like a kitchen racket more or less. An accordion ... and that's where I met my lad. Within two or three years after that I got married. I didn't want to get married and be poor. I didn't want to get married and not have heat in the house. There was no rush in getting married. We got married in thirty five. Then we moved in thirty seven to another apartment on the top floor. I had two children, two boys. We were three years married and living on top of a store and I said "I'm going to get ... we're going to buy a house." We got that apartment in Savin Hill. I lived out in nice houses you know and I said to the agent "I don't want no cockroaches." It was a nice apartment for twenty dollars a week, and twenty eight in the Winter with the heat.

I did stop working when I got married. My cousin was staying with us, a boarder, you know. He paid twenty dollars a week. You'd do the wash, the food and whatnot. But then in thirty eight we bought a house; a three family house, down at Fields Corner. I knew how to save. I knew bargains and my uncles and aunts had houses. Paying rent, you don't get nothing out of it. Looking at apartments it would be so dinky, and it stunk. I said I'd rather live on a cup of tea and have my own place because you can't go on in a place like that if somebody else don't keep it clean.

Raising a family in the thirties my husband worked every day, sometimes he had two jobs. We had seven children and they all did good.

I don't think I wanted to be married on the Aran Islands. I was forward, you know what I mean. It was opened up. I could go my way. Then there was mother-in-laws too. Some of the women got married there, that didn't want to. The parents would put them in sometimes. There was big pieces of land. Lots of girls did, I think. If I didn't get married I'd just live there, stay in the house with the brother, get a bite to eat and some clothes or something like that. There was some that stayed there. Oh yes, they used to tell us how they lived. It must have been terrible. But then they were happy too. Most had a great faith in God. I think that's what kept them going. Can you imagine mothers having one after another, kids ... ten, eleven, twelve? It was a hard life.

The States has been very good to us. The children have never been sick. Two nurses, one schoolteacher... When the children grew up I had moving out to here (Milton) on my mind. We had two houses in Dorchester, one rented out. Yes, I had a three family and five children in five rooms like this. (Only kept one apartment for entire family).

We never talked Irish to the children. Some raised their children here with it too. My sister used to write to me in Gaelic and it used to take me so long with the children so small. So, I started writing to her in English and she got the English to write back. Gaelic would take me a long time because it happens to leave your mind.

I enjoy work. Three hours I worked today (78 years old) in the high rise apartment. Work four days a week at housework, one of them on Beacon Street ... and I'm in the will. My husband, he's eighty two and working at Milton Academy. We don't have to work, but 'tis good. What would I be doing around the house? It's good for you.

Bridget McLaughlin - Donegal Woman

Bridget was born in 1905 in Creggagh, Carrenmullen, Malin Head, Co Donegal, one of the northern-most spots in Ireland. She came from a family of seven girls. They lived on a farm of fifty acres, and she attended the local schools until she was fifteen years of age. She was twenty when she decided to emigrate to Boston in 1925.

O n the farm there were all kinds of everything; turnips, cabbage, potatoes, and oats, everything. (The farm) was about fifty acres. We all helped out. We had to help out. I never went away anywhere to work. I thought it was great. We had a grand time at home, there was no need to leave there. But, other people didn't feel that way. Of course there were smaller farms.

My eldest sister got married and I was the next one - I decided to come. At that time, 1925, you had to have someone here in case anything happened to you. (I) had to go to Belfast and from there to the American consul. It all belonged to the Kingdom (UK) then. My own doctor gave me a medical check.

I came on the Cunard Line, *The Transylvania*, I think. Thirty two pounds or something like that (fare). That was second class. If you came steerage, you came third and you'd have to get off at Ellis Island. If you came second you didn't have to. There was a person from Detroit, Michigan, home in Ireland and I came along with her to New York. Then by train to Boston. The Traveller's Aid would put you on the train.

I was coming to Boston. My aunt met me at Boston. My aunts were over here. I used to address the letters for my grandmother. The one I came to was 5 Kenny Street, Jamaica Plain, Boston. My aunt Mary met me - she was single. She brought me to my aunt in Jamaica Plain. They were all married and had their families when I knew them. Their families were all grown up. Most of them were my age then.

I know when I came to Boston I didn't like it at all. Hated it in fact. I was accustomed to going to Derry quite a lot and Boston didn't seem all that better than Derry to me.

My aunt Mary lived in Groton. She was the head waitress at Groton School. I stayed for about a month at my aunt's and then I went to Groton. I didn't like it up there. On the farm (at home in Donegal) we had to milk cows, there was no machine. It didn't seem any different. It wasn't hard for me. I stayed all of three

months. I didn't like it there and I went to work in Brookline with
a family. A third cousin got me that job. I was cooking and
waiting on tables. Then I took care of their children for the next
four years. I stayed there until I got married. I got married from
there.

There were dancehalls at Dudley Street, but I liked the job
with the children so I wouldn't ask to do anything else. My
husband came to call on me when I came out. I knew him pretty
well, a Donegal man. He came to this country in March and I
came in August. He was studying as a stationary engineer at the
brewery. He did all that and then he got his licence. We got
married in June of 1930.

We lived for a short time in this country, in Dorchester, and
then went back to Ireland. Got married in June and went home in
December. They asked us to go back to our farm because no one
else wanted to stay there. They were all going to go. It was kind
of exciting, that was about it. That was in the time of the
Depression remember, so it wasn't very good here.

It wasn't a smart move. My husband, he wasn't really too
fond of farming because mostly he took care of doing the stores,
going getting stuff for the store. They (his family) had a store.
He stayed one year, that's all he wanted to stay (in Ireland). I had
two children born over there. I was pregnant when I went over
there and before he left the other one was on its way.

He went back and we didn't move (to the USA) until 1935.
They were two and three years old, the children. I just lived at
home. I didn't do anything. It wasn't hard because they were
crazy about the children. My husband got his old job back, and
stayed with his sisters. He bought the house and then I came. It
was the thing to do. That was what we intended to do, for me to
come.

I had to go to Dublin with the children, for the papers.
Leaving we went to Derry, Moville. I came to Fuller Street in
Dorchester. He had the house all ready. He always had plenty of
work. We lived next door to his sister. It was a two family house.
We always had it rented. That's where we lived up to when my
husband died. Stayed there until my daughter bought this house
here. Then I sold and came here to live with them.

The neighbourhood wasn't that Irish. Around us there were
very few like myself, that came from Ireland. There were mostly
all their grandparents came.

I've been over seven times (to Ireland). The change in the

new houses, they seemed to be doing much better. The young people had more money. Too much money I think. Now I wouldn't change, because I got to like it here. Things seemed to go alright for me. I travelled a little to Florida and Chicago. I enjoyed myself. I like to go back there for a vacation and that, but I'd never want to stay there now. My family is here now.

Bridie Halpin
"Up Us!" Profile of an Immigrant in New York

During the course of my work on *Models for Movers* I searched high and low for missing women who had been active in the revolution - unfortunately I could find no one. Bridie Halpin's papers/story were made known to me by Mike McCormick, *Irish Echo* and National Historian for the Ancient Order of Hibernians.

Never fear for Ireland
For she has soldiers still
Up us!
Bridie Halpin (1902-1988) *Jail Journal*,
North Dublin Union

Bridie Halpin was born and raised on Nichols Street above Christ church, in the city of Dublin on 14 April, 1902. A working woman and a revolutionary, she chose to become active in Cumann na mBan, the women's arm of the Irish Volunteers. Imprisoned at age eighteen, in 1923, for her Republican activities, she became the guest of the Irish Free State prison system first at the National Dublin Union (NDU), and later at Kilmainham jail.[6]

What emerges from the scant writings and letters of Bridie Halpin and the other women involved in the "struggle", is a somewhat hazy portrait of fighting women, strong in purpose, aware of their role in the political change of the time and their contribution in the fight for a Republic without boundary.[7]

The aims of Cumann na mBan emphasise the importance of equality in the struggle, placed second only to a separation from Britain.

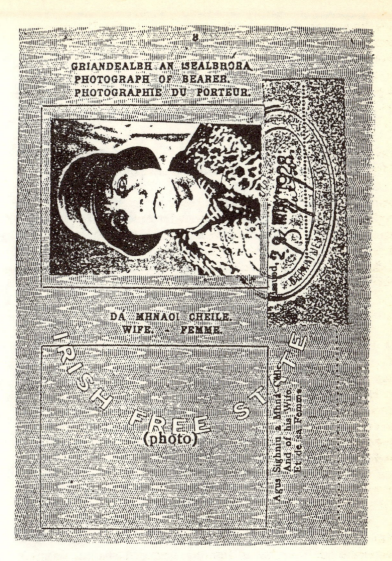

A page from Bridie Halpin's passport

The objectives were:

1　The complete separation of Ireland from all foreign powers.
2　The realisation of the declaration embodied in the Proclamation of 1916 guaranteeing Equal Rights and Opportunities to all.
3　The Unity of Ireland.
4　The Gaelicisation of Ireland.[8]

The significance of Bridie's life to this study is twofold: she was a revolutionary, committed to social change, and was deeply disappointed by the acceptance of the Treaty conditions which were in direct contradiction to the aims of the Cumann, and because of that she chose to emigrate. In America, she worked to bring about a "proper" settlement of Irish Affairs, work which was appreciated by other women leaders who remained in Ireland. As Maud Gonne MacBride who devoted sixty years of her life to "the cause" wrote to Bridie, "I see you are interested in our country as ever - There must be a lot to do for Ireland in America, to help us free our six still occupied counties we need all the help our own people abroad can give ..."[9]

Bridie's life as an emigrant provides a perfect example of a woman who decided to emigrate because she was dissatisfied with the society where she found herself and decided to attempt to change it from without. Abroad she hoped to continue her revolutionary work. In America, more than anywhere else, she wished to maintain pressure for change and gather support for the cause of an Irish Republic, free from any links with Britain and without a political border. Her vision of Ireland was by no means complete when she emigrated and her life's work would be spent attempting to realise that vision, albeit from afar.

Bridie died at Christmas, 1988, in New York city; she was 85 years of age. No rebel song glorifies her past. No obituaries were published on either side of the Atlantic for this woman with whom Maud Gonne MacBride corresponded and to whom de Valera sent annual Christmas cards. Her nephews and nieces, brought by her to the USA, were unaware of her past and were enlightened only when a suitcase of documents was found under her bed after her wake.

Far better the grave of a rebel
Without cross without stone
Without name
Than a treaty with treacherous England
That can only bring sorrow and shame.
Bridie Halpin - Kilmainham Jail[10]

As we trace Bridie's life we see the conscious development of a political mind, and a dawning of the concept "the personal is political." Her lifelong mission was to maintain support for the cause of a united Ireland and quite early on she identified the United States as the place where her energies could best be used to summon support both financial and political for the cause.[11]

However, as Bridie knew, support for the affairs of Ireland had dwindled greatly in the United States since the Treaty, which was perceived as the starting block for the new Ireland, and many interpreted this as the cue for foreign influence to exit. Undaunted, she applied for, and was given a visa for the United States in 1929. Her passport shows that a visa, no 27300 was issued on 27 May, 1929 by the American Consulate.[12] However, a further application on 23 April, 1931 was denied.[13] It may well be that evidence contrary to that supplied on her visa application came to light which may have revealed that she had been imprisoned. We know for certain that the quotas for that year went unfilled. Bridie did not apply again and instead decided upon a more surreptitious and lengthy route via Britain, Canada and eventually the USA. It took creativity, imagination and great persistence on her part to gain admittance to the United States. A letter from the Catholic Emigration Society to Bridie at her London address in 1937 states:

It will not be necessary for you to worry about passport or visa, these are not required for Canada.

She was assured that work of a "domestic nature" would be available.[14]

Eventually, Bridie was admitted to the United States on 28 July, 1946 a good seventeen years after her formal application and twenty years after her release from prison. She entered via Buffalo, New York and settled in New York city. There she formed a branch of Clann na Phoblachta, which was not terribly well supported.[15] She was also involved in the Choral societies right up to the time of her death.[16]

It is difficult to judge Bridie's success in raising American awareness to the unfinished business in Ireland, but suffice it to say that she continued her work in that regard till the day she died without ever revealing her revolutionary past.

"Maybe that's the sign of a real patriot."[17]

Mary Terry Kelly - 1920s Emigrant

Mary Terry Kelly/Máire Tríon Ceallaigh was born in Ring, County Waterford, a Gaeltacht area. She worked for several years in the Irish College there and decided to emigrate in 1923. In Boston she worked for many years as a domestic and cook. She married a "Yank" at age thirty and settled in Dedham, a suburb out the hub spokes from Boston. The interview was conducted in both Irish/Gaelic and English.

Máire Tríon Ceallaigh or Rinn ó Dhunagh, cuid de na Deise. Rugadh mé se bhliain is ceithre fichid ó shin. Bhí beirt sa chlann, mé féin agus deirifiúr Peig. Mise an duine is sinne. Bhíos ar scoil ar feadh seacht nó hocht bliana agus ansan chuaigh mé go dtí Choláiste na Rinne ar feadh bliain nó dhá bhliain is dócha. Bhí Gaeilge againn ansan ach ní raibh Gaeilge sa scoil naisiúnta.

Nuair a bhímis ag teacht ar scoil bhímis ag labhairt Béarla. Bhí Archbishop Sheehan ann ón Astráil. Tagadh sé gach aon bhliain go dtí an Rinn agus bhíodh sé ar buille má bhíod muid ag labhairt Béarla. Nuair a tháinig muid go dtí an tig in raibh Archbishop Sheehan thosnóidh muid ar an Gaeilge ansan. Labhair mo mháithir Gaelinn agus labhair m'athair Béarla. Bhí Gaeilge agus Béarla againn nuair a chuamis go dtí an scoil. Bhí Coláiste na Rinne dos na daoine a theastaigh uatha gach rud a bheith ag na páistí as Gaeilge, iad san a chuir na páistí ann.

Ansan bheadh na "Geibhrighs" ag teacht, daoine ó gach aon áit in Éirinn. N'fhéadar sin an ainm a bhí orhtu. Bhí uatha Gaeilge a fhoghlaim. Ansan tháinig na páistí agus bhí rince acu gach oíche sa scoil. Ní raibh aon Béarla againn i gColáiste na Rinne, Gaeilge amháin agus Francise agus Latin. D'fhan mé ann go dtí go raibh mé a ceathar deag. Ansan chuaigh mé ag obair ann, sa choláiste fein. Bhí mé sa chistín agus leis na leanaí. Bhí sé deachair, obair crua. Bhí an "Fear Mór" ann an uair sin. Tháinig sé ó Luimneach, Séamus ó hEocha. Tá mac leis i nGallaimh, Colm ó hEocha (uachtaráin Ollscoil na Gallaimhe).

Mary Terry Kelly
Photograph: Caitríona Cooke

Ní raibh morán airgead ann ag an am sin. Dúirt mé go dtiocfainn anseo. Dúirt an "Fear Mór" níos mó airgead a thabhairt domsa. Tháinig mé amach go dtí m'aintín agus m'uncail. Nuair a tháinig muid anseo bhíomar ag labhairt Gaeilge. Bhíomar ag teacht ar feadh seachtaine, ar bád, mé féin agus Eilís agus Máire, an triúr againn (cáirde lei). Bhíos naoi mbliana déag is dócha. Chuamar ó Corcaigh, Queenstown. Thug m'athair sinn. Bhí sé an uaigneach. Chuamar ar an mbád, Cunard Line, taille timpeall fiche punt (1923). (I lár an gcogadh mór) bhí daoine timpeall. Bhí aithne agam ar de Valera, Michael Collins, Pádraic Pearse ó bheith ag teacht go dtí an Choláiste. Bhí na "Black and Tans" ann. Cuireadar ceisteann orainn. Thuig me ansan an canúint a bhí orthu agus nar thanadar ón áit. We heard there had been an ambush. There was a fellow in the College by the name of Lysen and they'd children going there. He wanted me to governess with him. He was going to South Africa. I'd rather come to America than go to South Africa, so that's what I did.

Ní raibh mé anseo ach ar feadh seachtain nuair a chuaigh mé ag obair. Bhí cailín, Cáit (cara) ag obair i Hanover street agus dúirt sí go dtabharfadh sí job dom. Ach, ní ligeadh m'aintín dom dul mar dúirt sí go mbeadh sé níos fearr domsa dul sa tígh agus beith ag obair agus ag fanacht sa tígh - go mbeadh níos mó airgead ann. Sin a dhein mé.

I arrived in East Boston. They were there to meet me, to meet us. My uncle and aunt lived in Charlestown, 1 Wall Place. Then of course there were an awful lot of people from home in Charlestown. They had five children so they were great to take the other two that came with me because they had no place to go.

The first place I went was a Jewish place in Roxbury and my goodness I was starved there. I couldn't get back to Charlestown to eat a cooked meal. I didn't have any money at the time to go out and buy anything. They couldn't mix the milk dishes with the meat dishes; they were kosher, Russian Jews. You'd get a quarter of a pound of tea, last for a week. They'd have the tea, I'll never forget it, with a glass, which they do in Russia. My aunt came to see me one day and she saw. She said "You can't stay here." I gave my notice and left the same day, can you beat that!

I left there and went to the office again (employment). My aunt went with me because I wasn't long here. (The woman) said

"I'll take you, you have an honest face." It was out by Tufts College, West Somerville. I loved that place. I ate with them at the table. They had black coffee because of acute indigestion. It was killing me every swallow I took of it, and I thought I'd never get used to it. I was too bashful to ask for cream or sugar. They had two children, a boy and a girl. I took care of them and did the housework. I was with them two years until the other girl I came with called me. She was at Noble and Greenough school (private high school). She wanted me to come work with her there. I didn't want to give my notice. They had given me a raise. I got twelve dollars and Alice was getting ten at the school. I went out on my day off. I told Miss Mills (person hiring) I wouldn't come at ten dollars, I wanted twelve, and I got twelve. Alice said "Why don't I get it?" So, I said "Unless you ask you won't get."

There was a bunch of us. Every Saturday night there were - one from Armagh, Alice from Ring and her brother worked there, four Americans. We had lots of fun then dancing - Hibernian Hall and Decon halls. We'd walk fron Noble and Greenough school all the way along the Charles River and back again at night. On days off we'd go into town. Go and have dinner in the restaurant and go to a movie. Then we'd go to my aunt's. I sent money home, they never pressured me, but I always sent money home.

My family had a farm, very small and my father fished all the time out of Ballinagowan. In America I knew you couldn't pick up money off the street. I had sense enough for that. I knew you had to work for it, which I did. In summers then, when the school closed, we went to work in hotels in New Hampshire and Maine. Alice was with me there. We had lots of fun - Aspen Grill Hotel, Ogunquiet, Maine. I was pastry cook and Alice the vegetable cook. At the end of the summer the manager wanted me to go to Florida to this hotel there, but Alice wouldn't go, so, I didn't want to go alone. I went back to the school.

Then I went into the Back Bay, the New England Peabody Home (elite residential city area). I stayed there for almost ten years. The kitchen boy was from the north of Ireland, an Orangeman. Mrs Whittimore said "Do you mind?" I said "I certainly do not." I said "I'll get along with him if he'll get along with me." She said "You can only go to church every other Sunday." "Oh Mrs Whittimore" I said " I don't want it on those grounds. I'll take it on the condition that I'll go every Sunday, or

I won't take it." "Ok" she said. It was hard work.

I must have been thirty when I met my husband. I was at Noble and Greenough school. A girl from Armagh, she had a nephew with her, Frank, and he came up often with my husband. That's how we met. I wasn't anxious to get married. I worked with four others and we'd go to the dances every Saturday night. Thursday nights sometimes. So, we had lots of fun. Then after that I got married. I don't know. It must be 1933.

I went home to Ireland in 1932. Must have been my second visit. You could save when you were living in. You didn't have to buy as many clothes as a person that was working in an office or teaching or anything like that.

(I got married) and moved into this house, fifty two years ago. We rented and after that the house was for sale. So, we bought the house. I have two sons, one living in Maryland and one in Dedham (where Mary lives). Most of my friends are Irish. I also have Swedish friends, Lithuanian friends. Most of them are Irish-American. I called home last Sunday. My sister is in Ring. I write her every week and she writes me every week. I call about every three months.

Níl éinne anseo a bhfuil Gaeilge acu. Ta muintir na Gallimhe i Dedham. Tá aithne agam ar cuid acu. Ach, is deachair iad a thuiscint mar labhrann siad ana mear. Do theastaigh uaim an Gaeilge a thabhairt don clann, ach ní raibh aon meas acu air. Tá sé an deachair Gaeilge a labhairt anois mar níor labhair mé ar feadh trí fichead bliain.

Definitely life was better in the States though I love Ireland and I love Ring. You had more money and in Ireland you could never make any money. It's so sad today too they have good education. I miss the fireside chats, sitting around and the neighbours coming in. I miss Ireland. I love Ireland and don't let anybody ever say anything bad about Ireland as far as I'm concerned. Some people out here, they just forget about Ireland. I can't ever forget Ireland.

Mrs Bridgid Gilchrist - 1933

This history was sent to me on tape by Mrs Gilchrist. The story as she tells it has been transcribed verbatim here. The tape is in the O'Carroll Collection.[18]

At age of fourteen and one day, I sailed from Queenstown, County Cork in 1933. I looked down at the tender and I could see my mother and sister. I hung on to the rail and watched the last bit of Ireland disappear.

I was the youngest of ten children. The third son, John Kennedy, had to leave Ireland as the British were looking for him. He would travel miles away from Clonakilty and speak against the British. So, my mother brought her second son from England, he was working there. So, two sons left Ireland - John was sixteen years and two months and Michael was eighteen years. They came to Savin Hill in Dorchester and lived with their uncle. We did have an elder sister, but she died at age four and a half and my father died in 1929.

After John Kennedy my brother was on the police. He was married for eleven years, but had no children. They came to Ireland and he decided to take me back to the USA. We landed in NY on January the 27, seven days from Queenstown. I was not impressed, as I had been seasick all the way until I got to the Bronx and there I started school. I cried every night for two years. I had to sneak a letter to my mother. She replied she was coming to bring me back to Ireland. However, she had six sons and a daughter in the USA as they didn't want her to go back. So, even though she had one daughter back home in Ireland it was very depressing and no Irish could leave Ireland. Thank God for James Michael Curley for whom my brothers worked, (he) decided to get my mother a visa. And two years after I arrived, she arrived on Christmas eve. Now we had to worry about my sister. Again, James Michael Curley put up the bonds and said she would never go on welfare. And so shortly after my mother got here, my sister Mary arrived. My mother did not stay in New York but went to Boston and rented an apartment from her brother. When Mary arrived we had a great party and the whole family were here. I finally came to Boston and graduated from high school and after that I went to the Kearney Hospital to become a nurse. After three years I graduated and worked there. For goodness sake, I thought I was Florence Nightingale. Four years after I graduated I met a young medical student. He was graduating from Tufts medical school. I attended his graduation and met his parents. His father was a doctor in Springfield and he was Irish-American. His father, Bernard A Gilchrist, his grandfather, came from County Longford. Nine months later

Bernard Norbert Gilchrist MD and myself were married at St
Peter's church in Dorchester. He had to do his internship at
Boston City Hospital, no pay. So, I worked. He also did seven
and a half years more at no pay. I forgot to say a year after we
met he went to Ascension Island, he was in the Army. So, with
his cheques and my work and in 1958 we had our first son
named Terence, who I named after Terence McSwiney who was
murdered by the British. He was the Lord Mayor of Cork City.

I wanted more children. We finally came to Springfield and
bought a house and in 1953 I got pregnant again on Fool's Day. I
had my second son, Brian Frances. He attended Cranwell High
School in Lennox, Mass, and then Tufts University. There he
majored in Political Science. He wanted to be a politician I
guess. However, he changed his mind and wanted to be a doctor.
He went to several medical schools and after two years he went
to the Royal College of Surgeons in Dublin, Ireland. He had two
great years there, great training. Then he was accepted at Tufts
Medical School. He graduated in 1984 and now he has put in
five years of training and will be at Harvard Group next July
doing transplants at the Deaconess Hospital. The following year
he will go to St Jude's in Memphis, Tennessee. This time he will
do Paediatric surgery.

I forgot to mention the first son Terence. I sent him to St
John's prep school in Danvers and then to Assumption College in
Worcester. He went on to teach and then gave it up. He then
went into the bank and lives in Georgia.

I am just looking over things at night. When I went to school
in the Bronx the kids laughed at me. I guess they had never met
an Irish girl. Then I was so shy I did not want to read. I got over
that when I went to the nursing school. This is something else I
just thought about. When I arrived in New York I went to St
Benedict's school as I had a cousin there, Sr Anthony, who was a
Dominican nun, but it was quite far from where we were living.
So, my brother transferred me to PS71 and in fact when I arrived
first, Lordon Green, a friend of my brothers said "We cannot
allow this child to go through at this age called Bridgid as the
kids will laugh." So, they picked the Irish (English) for Bridgid
and called me Breda. Now I am sorry they did that because I still
love the name Bridgid. I'm sorry I gave it up.

After being at catholic school, the public school I went to,
PS71, then they put me in the colour guard and I had to carry the
flag. I did not know the pledge of allegiance nor the national

anthem which I finally learned.

After my husband was in practice in surgery we decided to go Ireland in 1957. My sisters took care of my sons. As I landed I felt like the Pope. I did not kiss the ground, but I had a great feeling as I stepped on it. I knew I was home. When leaving Shannon we were having a snack in the dining room and the thing that I remember, we were in Dingle the day before, and had heard that there were flights at half price going to the USA. So, as I looked out from the restaurant I saw fathers and mothers kissing their children goodbye. I said to my husband "They may never see them again." So, I had a good cry for myself. The waitress asked, and told, asked me...told me she wished she was going. On another trip we drove to Queenstown which is now Cobh and I told my husband to let me walk down to the place where I had walked in 1933. Again, I had some sad memories. We also took our sons to Ireland for a holiday twice. I have made twenty six trips myself. The last one was with my sister on a tour and please God I hope to make it again.

I am a member of the Irish Northern Aid for twenty years. In fact I had a fellow visit me ten years ago. He was in jail and on his ninth year. At Christmas time he was released and he was very grateful. He had five children who had received cheques from Northern Aid each month for which he was dearly grateful. I also belong to the Hibernians and I also receive the Irish Voice paper and the Irish Echo and the Irish People. I also belong to the Irish Cultural Society. I had forgotten, but I have found a clipping that I will send. My third brother Richard had apparently killed a few Black and Tans and was sent to Boston. So, after he left my fourth brother Andrew was sent to Cork city jail. They thought that he was Richard. The English police came to our house at midnight and grabbed Andrew, no hearing etc. I was about four years old. He was there for about eighteen months and finally he was off to Boston. He now has ten children in Boston.

I also forgot to tell you that I also belong to the Irish National Caucus in Washington DC. Fr Sean McManus from County Fermanagh had organised it and I gave him the first house party which raised several thousand dollars so he could go to Washington.

I guess that is my story. I am Breda Kennedy Gilchrist, 30 December, 1989.

Chapter Four
The Fifties Flight

Ar Re Dhearoil

*Tá cime romham
Tá cime i mo dhiaidh
Is mise fein ina lár
I mo chime mar chach,
Is a Dhia Mhóir
Foir ar na céadta againn
O d'fhágamar slán
Ag talamh ag trá
Tóg dá laimh sinn
Idir fheara is mhná
Sa chathair fhallsa*

Captives before and behind me
And I myself in the middle,
O Great God, protect the
hundreds of us,
since we said farewell to
land and beach
Take us in hand, men and
women, in this deceiving
city

le Máirtín O'Direáin a cailleadh mí Aibreain, 1988

According to historian JJ Lee, Ireland (the new Republic) in the 1950s had "the lowest living standards, the highest emigration rates, the worst unemployment rates, and the most intellectually stultifying society in northern Europe."[19] Like Máirtín O'Direáin, some individuals migrated within Ireland from rural to urban areas and hundreds of thousands emigrated. How could such a situation come about when Ireland had been free to determine its own course for nigh on thirty years?

The problems for Eire had indeed been mounting and following the disturbing decade of the 1940s the new Republic had little going for it economically. While northern Ireland was benefitting both from its inclusion in the British Welfare State and from increased industrial activity for the war effort, it finally had the psychological advantage of having been part of the force that stopped Hitler. As Churchill had assured Basil Brooke and the people of Ulster: "You carry with you my best wishes and the gratitude of the British race in every corner of the globe." More than anything its involvement guaranteed for northern Ireland a favorable place in the United States/Great Britain enterprise during reconstruction. Consequently, the position of women in northern Ireland could be expected to be somewhat different to that of their southern sisters during the decades which followed. Of significance also is the fact that southern Ireland had steadfastly held onto its neutrality, a necessary evil to "heal the wounds of the Civil war" (de Valera). The Irish population in general tended to side with the Allies though some links did exist between the IRA and the Nazis. With neutrality came imposed self-sufficiency, a national aim since the formation of the State, which Ireland had great difficulty achieving except perhaps in the matter of turf. But without a doubt the fact that Ireland had not been part of the effort to rid the world of this genocidal manic damaged the country's image considerably and was the cause of much suffering for emigrants, especially those in Britain.

The obvious organisational abilities built up over the course of Second World War and the uplifting experience of victory provided the British with the necessary tools for a positive recovery. The strength of the connection with the United States of America evidenced in the aid for Great Britain under the Marshall plan was most favorable to the rebuilding of the country. Ireland, at least the 26 counties, was disadvantaged considerably.

By exposure to a higher standard of living, the expectations of those Irish who had worked in Britain during the war were heightened. Men had been attracted into the armed forces and many women had answered the advertisments for work in armaments factories. The Commission on Emigration in 1956 reported that "Through the cinema and the radio, and above all by direct experience either personal or through relatives, people in such conditions are, more than ever before, becoming aware of the contrast between their way of life and that in other countries, especially urban centers." So great was the response that historian Terence Browne considered it an "outright rejection of rural life."[20]

The Atlee government in Britain, torn by a desire on the one hand to increase production in industry, and on the other to increase population, decided to pursue women vigorously back into the workforce with attractive posters and perks.[21] In footwear, clothing, laundries, iron and steel, transport and agriculture, cotton and wool textiles, women were asked to "Help make the goods we want. Join your friends at work. Put money in your bag."[22] The lasting social change and the choices that such enticement brought about in the late 1940s and the beginning of the 1950s is the most significant factor for the selection of Britain over America by women emigrating from Ireland in the fifties. In America, the post war response had been to get women out of overalls and back to motherhood.

This outward movement was enormous. Not since the 1850s had Ireland experienced such an outflow, bordering as it did on crisis levels. The numbers involved in agriculture in Ireland declined steadily as Britain's recovering economy was hungry for labourers, especially in the building and service areas. To remain at home was to join the ranks of the 78,000 unemployed (1957) and struggling to live on Unemployment benefits or assistance. Indeed the economy was so depressed that emigrants' remittances were recorded as part of the Gross National Product. However, emigration to the United States of America was minute by comparison with that to Britain since the chain had been broken in the 1920s when Ireland's quota for the USA had gone unfilled and few had been attracted to a depression- ridden New World in the 1930s.

In many ways, women were the real casualties of such a bleak and dismal economy. From the many corners of Ireland women disappear in the 1950s, driven by a rough and interminable lifestyle on farms to the freedom and opportunity of Great Britain, and to a lesser extent the United States.

The figures are indeed frightening when one considers that from 1951-1958 Ireland lost twice as many emigrants as it had since Independence, and levels hit rock bottom when in 1956 54,000 left the country. The total for the period 1951-1961 was over 400,000.

The Government's Commission on Emigration reported that because of massive emigration there was a need for a national population policy. Those on the Commission lamented the loss of the female domestic worker but could offer few definite proposals to ameliorate the situation. There were proposals to raise the status of housework or indeed tax all bachelors, ridiculous responses which pointed to the inability of the Commission to consider seriously the need for a solid economic policy to tackle Ireland's problems.

By the 1950s there were not enough single women of marriageable age to partner the farmers that needed them and areas in the west of Ireland were deprived of those who had formerly been content to lead the life of a farmer's wife. In fact "many Irish women preferred urban over rural styles even if it meant the possibility of being a spinister" (Kennedy, *The Irish* p 72). The result was an aging bachelor group, who, unable to find wives, died without leaving heirs for their land. Never since the days of the Famine had such a tragedy occurred in Irish agriculture. The emergence of the Lisdoonvarna fair - a matchmaking gathering with accompanying entertainment and amusements - reflects the desperation on the part of farmers to find partners, as do the writings of JB Keane whose central character is often the Irish bachelor.

Great Britain offered the young emigrant a modern welfare state which provided opportunities to men and women alike. For women, especially given the defeat of Noel Browne's Mother and Child Health Scheme, there was the added boon of unlimited free medical and gynaecological services unavailable in Ireland.

The United State of America presented a more permanent relocation and therefore the decision to emigrate there was more deliberate, perhaps even final. Not only would the move ensure employment but also greater power and independence than would have been available in Ireland. Deprived of suitable opportunities to marry, many an Irish woman decided to relocate. Of course many a woman was neither interested nor willing to consider marriage on either side of the Atlantic. If she did decide to marry in America she was free to choose whomever she wished without being concerned about dowry. There she could be an independent woman, and decide for herself what her role in life would be - a fate which she hoped would differ from the Ireland envisioned for her by de Valera in his 1943 St Patrick's day address, referring to Irish women as "comely maidens."

With internal migration many rural people married and raised families in urban areas. "Though economic trends and demographic patterns shifted the population to a more urban, eastern, profile, suburbanisation is perhaps the most significant change of the recent past. The proportion of the population dwelling in urban areas stood at 42% in 1951, and 46 per cent in 1961."[23] The lifestyle of the married urbanised dweller reflected a more definite division of labour than had previously existed on the family farm, and the position of women was even more clearly defined as one of housewife. The role of the women who lived on the many housing estates that were springing up around the city of Dublin, in Artane, Glasnevin, Lucan and so on, was to cook, clean, bear children and await the return of "himself."

In these times of economic downturn women were forced out of the labour force. If the lesson of the war years had told the women of the world that they could rivet as well as any man, the message of the 1950s was that they were to be delicate and always attractive for their men. For Irish women this translated into a push back into domestic work and a decrease in opportunities for any other form of employment in Ireland. It also appears that men were given preference and assured any industrial opportunities that existed.

The Mother and Child Scheme: The Litmus Test of Ireland's Commitment to Women

> The most serious revelation, however, is that the Roman Catholic Church would seem to be the effective government of this country.
> Editorial *The Irish Times*, 12 April, 1951

Nothing exemplifies Irish women's situation in the 26 counties more than the inability of one young Minister to take on the might of catholic Ireland in an attempt to legislate for the care of women during and after pregnancy. The "Mother and Child

Scheme" of Dr Noel Browne is a cornerstone in modern Irish history and an indicator of the might of both the catholic church and the loyalty of male politicians to the credo of the church.

The "Mother and Child Scheme" essentially concerned legislation which would benefit directly women in pre-and post - natal care. A concerted effort was made to successfully deter the enactment of the legislation. This legislation was blocked by the strongfellows of patriarchy, the church and parliament, and the ensuing public debate and private manouvering perpetuated an oppressive climate of opinion with regard to Irish women. The fiasco was one of the greatest disservices to Irish women and I believe spurred even greater emigration in the 1950s.

Estimated net emigration 1946-61
Republic of Ireland

Years	USA	Outside Europe	GB	TOTAL
46-51	15,875	3,506	100,187	119,568
51-56	13,975	7,956	174,832	196,763
56-61	24,842	12,854	172,307	212,003

Source: Drudy, *Irish Population Change*

A rejection of an increasingly hostile society and a desire to establish a better life in a society that offered more to women must not be discounted as either a conscious or unconscious motivation for a life across the Atlantic.

While having family connections in the USA was an important factor influencing the decision of those who decided to emigrate there, it was not the only one.

Originally introduced by Fianna Fail, the Health Act became law in 1947. This bill, amended by Dr Browne during his tenure as Minister for Health in the new interparty government of 1948, would provide "hospital, medical and surgical treatment for all mothers in respect of motherhood and of all children in all matters relating to ill-health and disease up to the age of 16." (*The Irish Times* 14 July, 1950) Both the catholic hierarchy and the medical profession objected to the Bill for many reasons. The medical profession feared the "socialisation of medicine", while the church was wary of the encroachment by the State into family matters.

> The establishment of this scheme [Mother and Child] would soon eliminate the free medical practitioner and create a monopoly of socialised medical services under complete State control - a terrible weapon to put into the hands of men who might not have received instruction in catholic principles, or who might repudiate such principles.
> (Dr Browne, Bishop of Galway, outlining the Hierarchy's opposition to the Mother and Child Scheme. *The Irish Times* 1 May, 1951)

The catholic Bishops in a private letter to de Valera in September 1947 objected to the terms of the Bill since "The right to provide for the physical education of children belongs to the family and not the State."[24]

The core concern in this letter, and in arguments ensuing in the debate that raged in 1951 between the church and Dr Browne, concerned the education of women in matters sexual.

> Education in regard to motherhood includes instruction in regard to sex relations, chastity and marriage...We regard with the greatest apprehension the proposal to give to local medical officers the right to tell catholic girls and women how they should behave in regard to this sphere of conduct at once so delicate and sacred......
> Gynaecological care may be, and in some other countries is, interpreted to include provision for birth limitation and abortion.[25]

According to the bishops, women's bodies were the concern of the church and not the medical profession. In this instance information for women was equated with control of their bodies and ultimately the possible destruction of the foetus. Is is of particular interest to note that in the debates that followed little was heard from women.

Pushed to the pin of his collar, Noel Browne wished to compromise, even though Part 3 of the Health Act of 1947, which had already become law on August 13, 1947, provided for the introduction of the Mother and Child Scheme. The church was adamant that the scheme was contrary to its social, not moral, teaching. As John Whyte, in *The Church and State in*

Modern Ireland 1923-1979, put it: "The real challenge being mounted by the hierarchy was their implicit claim to be the effective government." Therefore, a catholic ethos with regard to women's bodies was the ethos that would prevail in Irish society. The catholic ethos would ensure that Irish women were kept ignorant of the working of their bodies, unable to have access to gynaecological advice and birth control. The hierarchy requested that the government withdraw the bill. The then Taoiseach (Prime Minister) of the interparty government, John A Costello, assured the bishops that they could be guaranteed a favorable response and following Dr Browne's resignation Costello stated in the Dail

> I as a catholic obey my church authorities and will continue to do so, in spite of The Irish Times or anything else. Deputy Dr Browne was not competent or capable to fulfill the duties of the Department of Health.
> John Whyte, *The Church and State in Modern Ireland 1923-1979*

Browne, without the support of either his party leader or cabinet colleagues resigned, and the scheme was dropped. Sadly, Browne's tireless work for the almost total eradication of tuberculosis in Ireland was not sufficient to save him.

On 16 September, 1952 the new Minister for Health, Dr Ryan, met with the Archbishop of Dublin, John Charles Mc Quaid. It appears that Archbishop McQuaid demanded the elimination of the clause to "educate mothers in respect of motherhood." The central issue was exposed and following this a new National Health Council Law was passed in October 1953 after a meeting of episcopal and cabinet members.

Such was the response to the decision to drop the scheme that Sean O'Faolain was urged to write:

> In practice, the Hierarchy does much more than 'comment' or 'advise'. It commands.....When the catholic church, through its representatives, speaks, he [the Taoiseach] realises, and the Roman catholic public realises, that if they disobey, they may draw on themselves this weapon whose touch means death.
> "The Dail and the Bishops" in *The Bell*, Vol.XVII 3 June 1951

The blocking by church and state of the liberating legislation of the Mother and Child Scheme was a clear indication to women of the direction that Irish society was taking, and there is little doubt that as a result some women may have chosen to leave Ireland. Certainly, the massive unemployment and economic crisis discussed earlier were major factors. However, some women clearly realised that though the role of mother was venerated in Ireland, the practicalities of such a role were to be determined by the catholic church. In the 1950s it must have seemed that the future for women who chose to remain in Ireland was a bleak one on many levels, expected as they were to marry and produce many children at a time of great economic hardship. Many women at that time refused consciously or subsconsciously to bow to such a fate and decided instead to emigrate, to Britain especially and to further afield, more finally, the United States. Not until 1958, with the introduction of TK Whitaker's Programme for Economic Expansion, was there to be a dramatic change in Ireland's economic prospects.

One final choice open to women in southern Ireland especially was that of a life in a religious order. Nuns formed a major part of the church in Ireland and life within its ranks offered a measure of independence and security. As the only women-controlled institutions in Ireland, religious orders offered an attractive alternative to emigration. Into the ranks of the Mercy's, Dominican's, and Loreto's, flocked thousands of Irish women.[26.] The role of the religious orders in providing an alternative lifestyle for Irish women is a major area of study in and of itself. Interestingly, a "vocation" also provided the possibility of work abroad on the many missions that the Irish catholic church had established within its "religious empire" (McCaffrey) of the nineteenth century. Many women who joined religious orders were sent to the USA to minister to the needs of the flock in the New World, and become emigrants in effect, without ever having made a conscious decision to emigrate.

Eimear (Alias) - 1950s

(name withheld on request)
Eimear emigrated from Connemara in 1960, though she planned her trip in the closing years of the 1950s. She chooses to remain anonymous because of her views on catholicism and the fact that

"lots of my people are in religious orders." Her testimony is presented to reflect the experience of women in Ireland in the 1950s, and their possible reasons for choosing to emigrate to the United States.

Most women who emigrated from Galway came from small farms, not so Eimear. Her family had both land and a business, and were therefore more middle-class. She attended the local national school and later a rural domestic-economy school in Swinford. Her decision to emigrate at age seventeen was more a consequence of her desire to move to the United States, a pull, rather than a forced emigration or push.

'Twas growth, growth, growth all the way but I wasn't aware then that was what I was aiming for.

Born on 10 June, 1942 I am now 46 years, approaching the golden age of 47. My father was from County Offaly and my mother from Connemara. My father used to be a teacher. He came as a manager of one of those farmer's co-operatives. She (mother) was one of four. Her mother died when she was an infant in childbirth. She had an uncle and an aunt that were childless and they took her and she was reared there. She met my Dad, they got married and they had ten kids.

We were probably more fortunate than most people around there because my uncle had a business. We had a store and a farm. My mother was the sole heir of the place. She inherited a full business which was a bakery, a barroom and then we had another grocery store and a farm in Murvey. I was brought up with a lot of business background.

I was the seventh child and I suppose you could consider me the rebellious one. The rest of them went on to boarding school, and I refused to go. I only stayed at the rural domestic economy school for less than a year. I worked the business. I filled pints, milked cows, cleaned stables. I did farm work and the groceries. We had a travelling shop - weighed and paid and did all that. It was part of life. It was just the understood thing, and you did it.

You'd spend your day on the bog. Loading turf and shifting turf. You'd spend your day in the shop weighing sugar. At that time nothing came pre-packaged and at Christmas time you'd black nails from weighing currants and raisins and tea. You learned, there was a lot of knowledge. There were double standards in our house. The girls polished the boys' shoes, the girls milked the cows, and did a lot of the farmwork. The boys were primarily prepared for the business end of it. They might have gone into Galway to pay bills or to pick up extra supplies. Those double standards stayed with me for a long time and I carried them through my marriage until maybe the last ten years. So, I decided there was another side to a woman's role. I think there was a kind of a double standard with my father and mother too; even though she probably was a much more brilliant woman in her own right, he had the formal education, she didn't. Looking back I can see all of that now. She (mother) was definitely the worker and definitely the stronger of the two. She was the one who actually directed every ...she was the mother, the Irish mother. The Irish woman that actually appears to be very weak and subdued, but underneath it all (is) the strength of the whole family.

My life wasn't touched by it at all (the depression of the 1950s), and I have to be honest about this. We were merchants in the community and people came to us for their needs. There was an awful lot of credit extended. I felt very important. The biggest problem when I came out here was adjusting to not having that importance here. You were very important to the people because you gave a service. I think I'm service oriented from that.

There wasn't marriages taking place at the time. I was the up and coming generation that would be leaving. It was just an understood thing that anyone that reached seventeen, eighteen either did two things - they either went to England or they went to America. The majority of people would go to England, unless you were fortunate to have somebody to sponsor you to the States. The Mother and Child Scheme, I wasn't aware of that at that time.

America seemed to be offering the golden opportunities. Our idea of America at that time was to go and make some money, save it and come back and live in Ireland. It was a false dream. It wasn't like they were leaving forever. I only came over for two years. I was going to be transformed overnight by coming to America. Become a whole person - jobs and work and development, just growing.

There was great excitement when a Yank would arrive. They would arrive in all their finery and it was very impressive to a fourteen or fifteen year old who was running around in her bare feet. My sister came (to the USA) in 1949, she was getting married. She was living in Lynn and working in a department

store. She was eleven years older than I was so it was like
coming to an aunt. After a complete physical in Dublin, at the
American embassy and with the affidavit from the person who
was sponsoring you, you were on your way to the United States!
(Eimear flew from Shannon - Rynalla to Boston)

The streets were filthy dirty with snow. We left nine at night
and didn't get in till seven in the morning. I never cleared
customs, never cleared immigration. We walked straight
through. They called my sisters and said "Will you please send
her right back to the airport."

We went to live in Lynn. My first job was with CBS,
working in a factory. They were assembling some kind of
transistors. I worked there a very short time. My sister had a
friend that worked at Champion lamps, which was another
factory in Lynn. The money was much better, and I was
employed there. There were only four of us in the area. It was
very nice. There were older American women and it was hard
work, but it was enjoyable. It was an experience and I learned a
lot, but I was very lonely. I was homesick, very homesick. I
remember waking my sister one morning about three o'clock,
crying, begging her to give me the money to send me home. She
told me if I went back to sleep she'd give it to me in the morning.
Ha, I believed her. I worked in Champion lamps for two and a
half years. It was a very good job - a lot of money. I saved
enough, took a trip to Chicago, went to New York a couple of
times. My main ambition was to save enough to go home. I
suppose right there my life stopped growing. I had bought a coat
in Dublin and the coat was shortened according to the style in
Ireland at the time. When I arrived here the style here was very
long. I had all my clothes totally changed from what I had
coming. I didn't like that, again I resisted that. But I had no
choice. It was almost like I had submitted my whole will to the
way they were here. There was a great conflict between she
(sister) and I when I got here - to this very day. We have never
gotten over that because she doesn't quite understand that I have
more freedom than she had growing up. I saw things totally
different to how she saw them. I had a lot more exposure and I
was more secure in myself; even though I was probably insecure
I was a hell of a lot more secure in comparison to my sister. A lot
of my friends emigrated to Boston too at the same time. Some
went to New York, some to Boston, so there was that contact
between myself. We got into the Irish circle here. We were

pioneers (total abstinence association). We all joined the pioneers and were very active in the association and we'd take our outings. So, we had our own little social group here at the time. You must remember they had opened up emigration. There was a great migration of young people. From our own area alone there must have been twenty of us. We had an Irish dancehall down on Mass Avenue in Boston, near Symphony Hall, "The State Ballroom." We had the "Intercolonial" and the "Hibernian" and we had football teams and pioneer associations. Once I had my money saved, my goal reached, I headed home. I stayed home for almost a year. I was returning to the nest. It was a much freer life. You weren't as restricted. That's the difference between this country and Ireland. We're governed by the clock here. People don't enjoy life. It's all clock and time. I'm sure you're just as busy in Ireland and I mean, I worked probably just as hard in Ireland but I didn't have the pressure of that meeting the clock all the time that you have here - even in those days. I look back and make a comparison of it.

They have this insecurity that they have to work, and the job is everything. I have learned not to let that happen me now. But, this work ethic that they have has robbed them of a certain value, certain values of life. I believe that the majority of people that came in the 50s and 60s have still that with them, and they're not aware of it. The job, the job, the job. It can rob you of a more productive, fuller, more rounded life. The Irish were here and had to work hard to get that job. You must remember that the Irish, you can see the philosophy of it, that when they came first they couldn't apply. Now they were taking a place in society, and 'twas important for you to have that place in society. So, we learned that very soon after you got here. That ethic was very important. And prove yourself, you had to prove yourself.

I came back hoping not to stay any longer than two years again. But, that's when I met my husband, got married. I probably wouldn't be married to him today, but he had said that he wanted to live in Ireland. There was a common bond and an interest and I could see a future. He was an electrician and I could see myself with my business in Ireland. All these years in America when the children were young I had this idea that this would happen.

They were all living in Jamaica Plain, Dorchester, some in Brighton, but mostly Jamaica Plain. Then of course there were the domestic girls worked out in Brookline and Chestnut Hill.

Most of the girls I knew worked with John Hancock in insurance. A lot of Irish girls worked at Gillette, in the factory. The majority of them did domestic. It was for economic reasons if for nothing else, because they had a place to live.

My husband worked on the rural electrification. It was just starting at the time. My contemporaries that stayed there, these women are the mothers of the young kids that are emigrating now. There was a turn then. They were on the turn and their offspring now are going to be the real voice, the voice of Irish women.

Their mothers are the ones that made the turn, but they are the ones that are going to act on it. There's no pretence. They're going to take a stand in politics, in professional life.

I was twenty three when I married. He was twenty nine. We had gotten an apartment and set up house. We had two hundred dollars the day we got married, but we had all our furniture paid for. We paid for everything. If you didn't have the money, you didn't buy it; it was as simple as that.

Our first child wasn't born until two years after. We had put off having a family until we made that first trip (to Ireland) after we were married, to decide which way we would swing. He (husband) looked around for a job. I look back on it and realise he never really wanted to make that move. I became discouraged. Then our first child was born (1967) and fourteen months later the second child; a daughter and a son. In 1971 we went back to Ireland all four of us and he (husband) looked seriously to see if we'd go back. We decided we would, sold our house on the north shore and moved to the south shore and waited. His job at Shannon airport never came through. We'd wait for another few years. I realised that we were never going to go back.

The children had started school and I started to realise that (the move to Ireland) would never happen. That was a crisis in my own personal life because I realised that I had to do something for myself in order for me to survive here. What I did was I got involved in learning to be a travel agent.

I got a job with a travel agency filing. I'd go in for two hours while my youngest was in kindergarden. I actually worked for nothing, just to learn. I did that for almost a year and from there on I learned the business. Now, ten years later I'm working for myself, independent travel.

I took courses after the kids, English and computers, word processing and economics. My main ambition in life now is to go back full-time someday to school. I want to pursue that. That's my dream. That's the thirst now, the thirst for knowledge.

My oldest is going on to engineering, she's doing great and the other boy is doing public relations. She's very much a young woman of today with strong ideas and very much her own person. I wish that more Irish mothers would feel differently, give children that freedom to be themselves, to develop and grow into themselves and not be holding and controlling them. I think that's one of my biggest complaints about Irish mothers.

Dealing with issues like that (in psychotherapy) only comes when you're given the gift of search; not everybody is aware of that - there are things that you just can't answer on your own. I was fortunate that I had friends I could talk to. If I had stayed directly in an Irish circle I never would have grown to a point where I would have felt comfortable doing that (psychotherapy). I maintained a balance. I have a lot of Irish friends and a lot of American friends. My horizons were kinda broadened.

My husband had a very difficult time accepting the fact that I would even do it (psychotherapy). It's attitude. There's something wrong with you. There is something wrong with you if you're not happy with yourself and you're not dealing with emotions that are there, and you're confused about yourself. There is a search, to do something about it; not hide it and suppress it; but look for it and explore it.

I come from a religious background in Ireland, very religious, nuns and priests in the family. I'm a practicing catholic, but my view on the catholic religion... I believe in birth control, in family planning and I also believe you should have a free will. I'm very spiritual, but not very catholic. I feel our religion played an awful part in our suppression and our guilt. I gave the children a parochial schooling and that was strictly out of a sense of duty. I also felt that I wanted them to have exposure to other areas. I really didn't want them going to a catholic university. I felt that a broader education would help them develop exactly who they were, and make choices. My daughter is still practicing, she goes to church. My son doesn't. That's his choice and it doesn't upset me because that was the freedom I gave him. I believe he's going to be a better person and if his religion means anything to him, if it's of any value to him, he will come back.

I believe religion and spirituality is a very personal thing between you and your God, and I don't think it's something that should be stuffed down our throats. I think sometimes it was carried to an extreme.

I feel that a lot of old catholics have that here. There's a hypocrisy. So, it's power, a lot of power and guilt. God didn't want you to be guilty about anything. God wants you to be happy.

I think what happened in my life here truthfully is that I based all my happiness on going back to Ireland. I believed at the time the value was in the kindness and sensitivity (and) could only be achieved in Ireland. That was my thought as a young mother. As I became more aware and started to make changes in my own life here, get into the society, get into the way of life here, I realised that that could be achieved more here in a positive way. I became a lot happier here, but I also chose a way of life where I could be free and do what I wanted to. I did take control of my life. I had let my life be controlled by the decisions of my husband and based my happiness on what he would do. When I realised that wasn't feasible, I took charge and decided what I was going to do. I am only quarter way there yet. But I'm on my way.

Mary Walsh - 1950s

Mary Walsh comes from outside Galway city. Like many women before her she had to sacrifice her education to help on the farm after her father's illness. Her mother knowing the injustice of such an action, allowed her eldest the opportunity of emigrating later in the 1950s. Mary has hankered after education since and is now, in her fifties, taking computer and word processing courses. However, she and her husband have ensured that their two daughters have a good education. One attends Harvard and the other Brown, both considered to be Ivy League Universities.

I 'm from three miles outside Galway city, Killtollough, Oranmore. Born in 1937, I'm fifty one years old. There were six in the family. I was the oldest. I went to primary school. I never worked in Ireland except around the house and the farm. It was forty five acres; we grew oats and corn, sugar beet, and we had animals, but we didn't have a dairy farm. We had two cows gave ourselves milk. My father was sick, so I was kept from school for that reason. My mother felt that was an injustice so when a cousin came home and visited she gave me the opportunity of going to America.

I actually thought hey, without an education where do you go from there? This was the first real opportunity and I felt I'd try it anyway; I won't let it go by. That was the only reason I came. There were actually two from the village there, but they went to California.

I went to Dublin to the Consul, that was the extent of my travels though I'd been to Cork with the Legion of Mary. I was early in the Pioneers, the Sodality and the Choir and all that.

I expected to own a house, which is true too, you know. I had always heard that before because housework was generally what we did, not having an education. I had no idea what else I could do.

I flew in 1957. The most mysterious thing was coming through the Callaghan Tunnel, that still stays with me. My grandaunt sponsored me. She lived on the Fenway, on 133 Peterborough Street, in Boston. It was an apartment building with a green canopy over the door. I thought she owned the whole building, but she didn't, she just owned a little apartment. On Sunday I got a job in Brookline through friends of hers. They were a catholic family and there was a cook there from Gort. So, I was lucky I was made very comfortable. I worked a full six days. I wouldn't say it was hard, I was taking care of kids. There were four children. I'd start in the morning at seven, get them ready for school. I did put the clothes away and take care of the rooms and the second floor. It was nice and comfortable, just very nice. We went to Hyannisport for the summer. I used to take them to the beach, they were all out of school then, and I couldn't even swim. But, there was a life guard on the beach, a private beach. I'd be laying out down on the sand and thinking of them at home weeding. I used to do the weeding at home and you'd get those things on your hands from weeding. I was working of course, but laying down. But it wasn't hard work, no way. When you live-in it's a little easier, but you have a longer day. Of course you're babysitting if the family goes out. But it's a long day for forty dollars a week.

In the wealthy neighbourhoods everybody kept help. In the first job I had there were six of us close by and where I worked welcomed any company. You could have the kitchen and make tea. The cook was old, she never went dancing. I went to The Hibernian at the weekends. There was plenty of opportunity to meet friends on Saturdays and Thursdays; dance night, ball games, also, at the Mission church on Wednesday night.

I was here three and half years and I made a trip home. It was in 1960, the year Kennedy got in. I remember it was over the radio in the morning at home. My mother said "Why don't you stay till after Christmas?" and I did.

After that I didn't do kids. Not that I didn't like it but you're not as tied down if you're cooking. It was a nice break for the first family and you felt protected (they) being catholic, there was nothing different about it. The money wasn't great, but it was all yours. Cooking I got fifty dollars.

When I came back I got another job. Somebody else I knew. There was always somebody, it was easy to find work. I worked there for nine months and got married. I met Michael at a wedding, the second day he came to the country. He's Galway, close to Oranmore. I knew him for four years. I was twenty seven when I married.

We bought a house in Dorchester. I came in 1957 and I got married in 1964. He came in 1959. So, we bought a six family house. We lived in one of the apartments of course and we rented the others. Michael had his own business, a mechanic. Four years after we were married we bought this lot of land and built this house (in Milton). We also had our first child that same year.

You have to think. The six family (house) was a good way of doing that because you had an income. It carried the mortgage. It also went a good way towards the mortgage on this house. I think if you're born in a farm that's all you think about. Especially being the eldest. I don't think I'd have gotten that far in Ireland in the thinking and planning and that. It took me seven years. Four thousand would buy a house. Houses cost forty or thirty eight thousand and you need four thousand to put down. You'd need a lot more to put down today. We were better savers, we were afraid. We saved because we were afraid. I do think too that having an education, you're more secure than if you don't have an education; we didn't.

I took my sister out later and she was a secretary. The only thing I had to have to bring her was two thousand dollars in the bank. That's all, then you could claim her. She lived with us here for a while, for a long time, eighteen years. She hasn't married. She's working in a lawyer's office. Michael had a cousin and two friends stay. It's a new ball game for us to be alone.

We're friends with neighbours, as neighbours, but close friends are Irish: Kerry, Cork, Mayo and Galway. We're more comfortable with each other. I'm really not that curious about other ethnic groups. We have the same thing in common, music and dancing. I've joined the Eire Society and the Social Club in West Roxbury. A group of us, six or seven couples, gets together every Saturday night, men and women, and we go out dancing. We don't generally go to bars. We go away and get a table and dance.

I took typing and I realised that I had to take English. You need an English course for the grammar. I do Michael's books for the repair shop. It was my own time and we have an accountant.

My family has a phone now, letters were the main form. My mother is living though I'm not a good one for calling. That old thing stays with you, the expense. Even though you might spend it foolishly otherwise. Also, my mother wasn't that good on the phone. She likes a letter.

My second girl is at Brown in Rhode Island and my first at Harvard. Well, of course, I don't think you can beat an education. I hope they get a good job, but if they don't I still feel that would be a legacy to anybody to be well educated and well read. You just enjoy so many more things. I wouldn't be interested in going back to school. I'm too lazy. You can tell your kids to study, but don't tell yourself to sit down.

I enjoy church. I don't have any objection to you if you don't want to go to church, and I'm not going to tell you or that kind of thing. It's a private thing. It's nice to have somebody else to talk to, if nobody wants to listen.

There's nothing dull about life here. When you're willing to work, you're content to work to keep it together for the weekend. Maybe the going out of a Saturday night with the friends kept us going.

Frances Newall Coen - 1950s

Frances Newall Coen works as a Public Relations person at the John F Kennedy Museum, at Columbia Point, Boston, Massachusetts. She had "this passion to leave Ireland" and that she did on the day of her eighteenth birthday, bound for Boston. Widowed ten years ago in 1979, she raised her six children alone. Throughout her life she has been involved in Democratic politics, "the working man's party" and has worked on the campaigns of many State and House representatives.

I was born in 1937. My village was Kilmurvey, Headford, County Galway. There were nine children in the family, five girls and four boys, I'm eight. Nine children in ten years and there wasn't any money.

Education wasn't free. It was a pound or two pounds every three months for secondary school. Most people didn't have an opportunity to go to secondary school because they simply couldn't have the money. I was robbed of that. Now it's free education and they have a tremendous educational system. I honestly believe the worst thing in the world is to waste a mind. You didn't get the opportunity. You also didn't get the encouragement from your parents because before them they had the same background. There was no one there to tell you it's important. To be honest with you I think most of my education is in the United States. I'm self-educated really.

I resented the class distinction in Ireland. I feel that it marked a lot of us, and I was one. I was able to overcome it but in school we were taught by the sisters we were not important as people. My work in school was not important, but the lawyer's daughter, the doctor's daughter, the bank manager's daughter was important. They were all in the front of the class. They were the people picked to stand in front of the class and read their composition. They (the nuns) probably never said it verbally, but you just knew "well you're the farmer's daughter so it's not important." That really bothered me terribly. It was expected that you'd be going nowhere (except) to marriage. I had no intentions of ever getting married and I think that's why so many people emigrated to America.

I went for two years (to secondary school) then I went to live with my sister in Dublin. I worked in a factory, a shirt factory - hated it. I was planning on coming to the States. I had decided I was coming to the States when I was twelve. I knew there was nothing for me in Ireland. Women had to cater to men. That's how it was over there. I remember on Saturday evening it was my job to polish and shine all of my brothers' and my father's shoes for Sunday morning mass. You had to work on the farm, but no matter how tired you were, you still had to do your house duties, because you were a woman, and that had to be done. I could not wait till I was eighteen.

My sister Mary is six years older than me and when I was twelve she was talking about going to America and she did go at nineteen, in 1950. I just knew I was going to join her, and I did. We were very close when we were young. We had that very special relationship very young. When she left for America I told her "You know when I'm eighteen I'm going to be over there with you." I had this passion to leave Ireland.

My mother's sisters and brothers were in Boston. They were a very tight, close family and they used to write to each other a lot. They used to send clothes home to us and I always loved the smell of that box. The excitement when a box would come from America. I remember hunter-green pants. I was dying to wear slacks, and it wasn't allowed. I used to put them on in my bedroom, but I could never come out of the bedroom, because my parents would kill me.

My sister and a brother were here before me. I came out to my sister Mary in 1955. At Shannon airport I don't even remember crying. Mary worked as a cook on Lee Street in a private home. I stayed with my aunt in Brighton for a month. My family, my cousins they were just wonderful because they made me feel like I was the most special person in the world when I came here. On that night (first night in Boston) I was introduced to forty cousins. It took me a month to climatize myself to this country. My brother Michael had a big group of friends and he introduced me to all of them. I had this wonderful social life. We went to Hibernian Hall, Colonial Hall. I wasn't long in the country and I won Miss Hibernia. My first job was on Reservoir Avenue in Chestnut Hill for a family. They had three children and I was hired as a cook, at thirty dollars a week. Of course I didn't know the first thing about cooking, but I tell you, she taught me well.

I lived there and had Thursdays off after I got breakfast, and a half day on Sunday. We worked very hard, because they entertained a lot and I'd be working until eleven at night sometimes. I stayed with them two and a half years then I worked for a Jewish family in Brookline. I had had it at the Brickleys (first job). It was very confining with the children and I wanted to make more money. I had met my husband in 1958. So, I went working for the Kruegers. I got fifty dollars a week.

I was married in October of 1959, (after) two years dating. I was twenty two and Tom was twenty five. Our first apartment was in Dorchester and then we bought a three-family house eighteen months after we were married. It was a thousand dollars down. So, you saved and saved. This three-family house in Dorchester, the rents were almost covering the mortgage. We kept that for three years, sold it and moved to West Roxbury.

In 1972, the year of the bussing I had four children in school and we decided, "we're going to sell the house." And we loved our home, but we had no other choice. I didn't want my children going to schools if they couldn't go to their neighbourhood schools. I didn't want them to be going in different buses and I certainly didn't want them, to be frank and honest about it, going into neighbourhoods that I wouldn't go into because it was dangerous. The whole idea of children travelling ten or fifteen miles to school was ridiculous. By the time they got there they were so hyper and upset. It was just no way to educate kids. So, we decided we had no choice. My late husband worked in a wholesale meat distributors from the day we met until the day he died of cancer in 1979. I know what I've lost and I know what it is to be alone. Tom, he was the kind of a man who wanted to spend time talking to me at night-time. It was important that the kids went to bed at nine thirty so that him and I had a couple of hours. But we had a tendency to give a lot to our kids.

They knew how sick Tom was. We went through two tough years of Tom's illness, but we talked. We'd sit at the table and talk. I had tremendous support from my family, brothers and sisters and I have the greatest family, my kids. My oldest had just finished her first year in College, my youngest was three. I supported them and they supported me. There were times when I was totally frustrated, worn out, but somehow I knew I was a strong person. Tom always told me I was strong.

I got over Tom's death and I went on and I got up. That's what you have to do if you really loved that man. He left you with six children and you two had all those plans for those kids. I used to have talks with the kids and I'd say to them "There will be one parent in this home, one disciplinarian, that's it." If I made mistakes, I'd be responsible for them. If they turned out good, they were my six million dollars. "I'm going to call the shots." I've had a lot of compliments given to me about my children and given to my children about me, and I'm proud of that.

My religion is very important to me and I've instilled it into my children. We weren't pious or preaching or anything and I could respect that if I had a friend who never saw the inside of a church, that was nobody's business but that person's. But to me you can't be a good catholic until you first learn to be a good christian. That's most important. In Ireland they taught you how to be a good catholic but forgot about being a christian.

I knew he (Tom) was very much into education and I was very much into education because I was robbed of it. All the children got College education, all four of them. My son Michael will graduate high school and go, and then the baby. The rest are all quite successful.

I've been at the JFK five and a half years. I applied with no experience but I had worked with a parish group to see what we could do with the divorced, widowed and separated. I said "Why don't we have a dance?" At a meeting a woman said "Fran, you know there is a position available at the JFK Library and I keep on watching you and thinking you'd be wonderful for that position." I had absolutely no résumé. I got the position and I cried for two days because I didn't have Tom to share it with. I was the happiest woman in the world. I love it, I absolutely love it.

I've always been good with people and I've always been involved with politics, working a lot on campaigns in Boston. Newman Flanigan, the Suffolk District Attorney, Joe Mokeley who's our Congressman, Arthur Lewis who is my State Senator, whom I still work for to this day and now Joe Kennedy. I haven't voted anything else but Democratic. I believe it's the working man's party. I volunteered. Well, men might have been in the smoke-filled rooms, but you had a lot of contact with the public. I was coordinating coffee hours, getting the candidate there, calling people and getting them to stand at street corners holding signs. Politics is really the grassroots. If a politician doesn't go door to door, and he doesn't shake hands, forget it, you're not going to get elected. When I was a very young child in Ireland I remember being so excited when the politicians would come to the square on a Sunday during elections giving speeches.

I don't have enough education myself but I have three sons and I will probably live vicariously. Kevin my eldest boy is in politics, a legislative aide, and he's very much involved and so too is my youngest lad. I'll get them there.

Irene McKenzie - 1950s

Irene was born in Cork city, on Patrick's Hill. She went to the local school, St Angela's, and later the Ursuline convent in Blackrock. She studied Science at University College Cork and married at 21, the year she was to graduate. She emigrated with her husband, initially to Toronto in 1957 and returned to Ireland in 1960. The family then emigrated to Boston in 1963. She has lived in Boston since. She is the only one of her family to have emigrated.

My father was a lawyer, and there were five girls in the family; I was fourth. I went to University College Cork in 1951. It was great, 'twas marvellous. I was at a boarding school and it was all girls and then I got into all these guys. It was just heaven. It actually took me four years (to complete the BSc) because I goofed off the first year.

It really was a very nice time growing up then because you didn't have to work. It was very safe to go anywhere. There were no restrictions. I led a very sheltered life, because when I was at boarding school I didn't see anything except the nuns, and you certainly didn't hear anything about Noel Browne from them. I wasn't really interested in that (Mother and Child Scheme), I was interested in enjoying myself.

The prospects for work were not too good. I got a job teaching in Bandon Grammar school. It was a Protestant school. I taught three days a week for five pounds a week. There were no other jobs around. I applied to the factory in Mallow and I didn't get in there. I didn't have any intentions when I graduated. I fell into the teaching job.

My mother was totally opposed to it (the marriage). It was such a hassle at home listening to this "na, na, na" all the time. The guy I was going to marry was lower class. I can see now where she was coming from. He had never gone to College or anything like that. He was seven years older than me too. I got married in February and I graduated the following September.

Irene McKenzie
Photograph: Caitríona Cooke

After that I taught. I was three years married when I had the baby and then I went back. I taught until 1957.

We came to Canada first. My husband wanted to emigrate. He had been in England and had an aunt in America. He always wanted to come out to the States. I guess I felt ok because I came. I hated it there. I was very lonely there. Toronto was a very nice city but at that time with the baby and not knowing anybody, I couldn't wait to get home. We stayed three years and I worked at the University in the Botany Department.

We went home and my husband decided to open a pig farm. 'Twas Christmas of 1960 and my second child was born in April of 1961. I was living with my mother in Douglas. He used to travel out to Macroom every day. It was a foolish kind of a thing really, because how can one person run a pig farm? I had two kids and I wasn't going sloshing around looking after pigs. That petered out and we came here (Boston) in 1963, you had to do something.

I probably didn't have a big huge say in going to Canada or Boston. We came by boat to New York, sailed out of Southampton. It was a ghastly trip. The little fellow was getting toilet- trained. Oh my God! He used to drive me nuts. Every minute he used to say "Toily, toily." Really, if I could have jumped overboard I would have. It was tortuous, really tortuous. We arrived and the suitcase handle fell off. This guy in the train station he gave us a piece of string and charged us two dollars for it. What a rip off. He saw us coming. We stayed at the Essex Hotel in Boston. Then we got an apartment in Dorchester; a furnished apartment, dreadful place.

We moved out of Dorchester to the South Shore, Brockton. We bought the house in 1968. My husband worked in a chemical factory in Cambridge and then in Polaroid. Then in 1972 he had a heart attack and open heart surgery. He never worked after that. I worked at the Deaconess Hospital doing cancer research. At that time, grant money was plentiful then and when that stopped I came here (New England Medical Centre).

I've worked all through my married life. To say it's unusual is an understatement. Number one, I didn't know anybody only myself that got married in College and two, they didn't work when they got married. I managed somehow. When he had the heart attack the small fellow was ten and the girl fourteen. It was the pits. Also, there was the added problem in that my husband was an alcoholic. So, he just drank away. The disease got worse.

I don't think emigration had anything to do with it; the same thing would have happened at home.

I didn't look upon myself as a martyr or anything like that. I had friends but it was not like it would be at home. Everybody was an emigrant out here, and everyone had their own problems. What are you going to do? Go "na, naing" to them? The marriage actually lasted too long. We got divorced in 1984. I should have done it a long time before that. I probably wouldn't have done it only he was in this hospital here; all the doctors, the psychiatrist, the Department of Cardiology, everybody was pushing me. He was really out of his mind. I had a lot of support from places where I really didn't expect it. In the end, it didn't matter if I was an Irish catholic or not, it got so bad I really didn't have any choice.

Nobody at home went into cardiac arrest (over the divorce). There was none of that stuff because I think everybody knew what my mother knew; probably what I knew too, only I wasn't looking at it. I stayed that long (in the marriage) because I didn't know anybody that was divorced in Ireland. They do now. You know, it was bashed into you when you were a child to stay. It was no good for me. It was terrible for the children and it probably was not good for him too. Probably if I was married at home I would still be in it.

It was the pits. But I didn't look upon myself as a martyr. I guess it (spiritual side) was my strength. If you are married to an addict there is no marriage. I went to a priest, a friend from Cork. I just didn't make this up myself. I could have gotten an annulment, but it was so awful; I really didn't want to drag it all up again.

I never knew what normal was. I get picked up now. I work in Boston and my (second) husband works in Norwood. I get dropped off at the train station and picked up every evening - and that's normal. Before, I could be waiting at the train station till the next morning.

The children are twenty eight and thirty two. One is a nurse and the younger fellow, he's not through with school yet. The drinking really affected him. It affected them both very badly.

I didn't look on myself as a divorced Irishwoman. I was just so relieved to have this weight lifted off my shoulders. I met my (second) husband on a plane. He works with the airlines and I was just sitting next to him. It isn't that I was out looking or anything, I can tell you that; absolutely the last thought on my mind. He's very nice. I knew him a year and then we got married. He's very normal.

I didn't tell anybody, but I guess everybody knew. My first husband sold the house then went home. It was sad really. He was like Lord Gough; renting cars, buying all over the place. He just dribbled all his money away. He's back here now, not a penny.

I always went home. My (second) husband is American and when I used to go home I'd stay with my sisters. When (you're with) Irish people, they talk about Irish stuff. They talk very quickly and non-stop about all the things that happened, it really wasn't fair to him. So, I said it would be nicer if he had his own place. We bought a house over there in Crosshaven (Cork, Ireland) and go over three or four times a year - and it really is gorgeous. He can potter around the garden and I can run up to Cork and have lunch with whoever. I don't think he'd pack and go forever, but he loves it over there, and I do too. When I'm there I forget about here.

My advice (to young Irish women) is be sure they can support themselves. They need some kind of education, or some kind of training. I wouldn't advise anyone just to come here with nothing - that's disastrous. Where would I be if I had nothing?

Eileen Newell - 1950s

Eileen hails from Carandonagh, Co Donegal. After twenty years in the USA she still speaks with a delightful Donegal lilt. Eileen, forced by poverty, decided to emigrate in 1959. She and Mike belong to a group of six Irish couples, avid ballroom dancers, who have met every Saturday night in Boston for the last fifteen years.

I was born July 12, 1940, that makes me 49. Christened Ellen T O'Donnell, but I ended up getting Eileen. I come from a family of ten. My father died when I was young. We were farmers, poor farmers - mostly potatoes, turf, hay and milking cows. Everyone had their own job. I came second. They said I bossed them around and I was mean.

Eileen Newell
Photograph: Caitríona Cooke

All the boys went there (Scotland), that's how they would make their money. There was about fifty children in the area and three teachers for the whole school. With no money, we had to stay out of school a lot to work on the farm, so they used to come looking for us to see where we were. We were very poor. It was tough, but everyone around us was in the same boat.

My mother was an American citizen. She was born in Montana and her mother died at her birth. Her father died three years later and an aunt from Ireland came out and took her back to Ireland. She stayed in Ireland till she was eighteen. She came to Botosn in the 1920s and stayed in Winchester. She lived there for about four years and went back. She ended up marrying my father. He died with noone to turn to.

From her I got the information (on the USA). The boys (went) to England and the girls to Boston. She just thought it was a great place. I think she was sorry she didn't stay. American work was easier for a woman and better opportunities.

I came in 1959 with my sister Bridie. I was eighteen and Bridie sixteen. We came over to live with a brother of my father. My uncle sent us the fare and we paid him back later. He lived in Dorchester, at 179 Milton Street. (It was) two weeks before I started working, taking care of children in Brookline. Thirty dollars a week for a Jewish family. You just learn to do what they like, you got used to it.

My sister worked nearby and you were never lonely because there was other Irish girls around. I got out of there and went to work for a doctor minding children.

On Thursday, our day off, we went into town, spent money and went dancing. Wednesday night we'd go to Mission Church for the Novena. Hopefully we'd get a date. The worst thing to do was to be seen in a pub - real cheap.

We met (husband) at the Stella Ballroom and got married in 1963. I continued to work in a nursing home and came home in the evenings. We lived in a three family in Dorchester for two years then bought a house in Milton. (We had) two boys, Michael and Sean.

There are lots of Irish around here. Six couples get together on a Saturday night (to go dancing). A great friendship. Nice people.

Every other year I go back to Carandonagh. We have a second home in Galway. Mike goes every year and I usually skip a year. But from now on I'm going every year. The homes are beautiful, life is so much easier. It's changed for the better there. In another ten years I'll live there. When I'm there I'm happy, but when I'm here I'm happy too.

My advice, get a good education and a job, then it is easy. (This is a) great country to get married in, and have children. I'm happy and content.

Chapter Five
The Interim Years
The 1960s

Terry Ryan Ryder - 1960s

Terry Ryan Ryder was born in the Liberties of Dublin, a well know working class inner city area. She suffered early from TB, and was moved to a sanitarium aged eight. There she was expected to die. Instead she read her way into autonomy, sprang back into the world and began a work life aged eighteen. Terry emigrated to Boston in the 1960s. She married Ken Ryder when she was forty and they have two children. Though her formal education finished in national school, Terry graduated with her BA from Northeastern University in the summer of 1988. She was then fifty two years of age.

I was born in Dublin in April of 1936. I was christened Catherine Teresa Ryan, but because there were twenty seven thousand Catherines in the family, naturally noone called me Catherine. I have two sisters and one brother and none of them use their given name. They use their middle names.

I was born on a street that no longer exists. I believe I was born on Beaver street, somewhere off Sheriff Street. It was an old Dublin tenement, one of the old, probably Georgian, houses. So, that's where I started out. I don't even know where that is any more - it's been levelled. Then we went to live in a block of flats called Liberty House Flats. We moved out of there again during what they considered the slum clearing project. Also, by virtue of the fact that I had TB when I was a young child. People who got houses in the suburbs were ones who had children who had TB, they got preferential housing. That's how my mother got the house in Dunkerin. I was supposed to have a room to myself because at the time it was contagious, and it still is, but they had no way of controlling it.

Up to that point we were living in this flat in the Liberty House Flats and it had one bedroom. I don't even have strong memories of that flat. I know in my mind what it looks like, but I don't remember any great deprivation, but I know that it must have been terribly crowded because there were five of us living (there). At some point my father must have been there too, although he died before I can remember him. So, six people were living in a one-bedroom, livingroom, kitchen type flat. It did have the modern conveniences that they didn't have on Beaver Street which was gas stove and running water.

My father was a soldier in the Free State army. While professionally he was apparently on the up and up, and he was a very bright man, he just couldn't support a family of four. He ended up as a day labourer in England during the War. He would come home whenever they could afford to get home, which wasn't very often. Because of the wartime regulations it was less likely that he was able to get home. He got pneumonia and I suspect was very malnourished because he sent any money that he had home to support his wife and kids. He died of pneumonia in England during the War. Because of wartime regulations my mother had to go and visit him in England and went through the Blitz in London. He died in a London hospital and they wouldn't let her bring his body home to Ireland. They said it was because of wartime regulations. She being a woman who didn't fight the system much didn't question that. I'm sure it was a legitimate claim, but his body has never been returned to Ireland. He's still buried in England.

I think I probably had TB for a lot longer than was actually established. I think they did not detect it until this mass screening of people came into being when it was perfectly obvious that the disease was epidemic. Then the government stepped in and started doing mass screenings of families. I can only assume that I was a placid child because I was always tired and that's the mark of the disease. I wasn't a high energy level child. When other kids were out playing on the streets I would tend to be reading. I went to Rutland Street School which is not high on the echelon of schools in Dublin. I made my first Holy Communion at that school and I did well in school. I did well because I could read before I went to school, as my brother could. My parents were both not very well educated, but very literate people. In

today's educational standing I would consider them very
educated people, not necessarily formal education, but their
depth of knowledge and their breath of interest - my father sang
opera. I went to Rutland Street School until I was probably about
eight. I left formal education somewhere between the age of nine
and ten. I know I got as far as third class, but I doubt I got very
far beyond it. That's the last time I went to school until I went to
college at Northeastern.

They told my mother that I would have to be hospitalized.
Now again the methodology in Ireland healthwise was obviously
very good, they set out at least to determine who had TB, and
what should be done about it. In my particular case they sent me
away to a place called Peamount which at that time had a
children's wing. I was with children from all over the country.
That was a great hardship on my mother because she had no
transportation and it was quite a distance for her to get to. I got
no treatment there at all and very little supervision. We used to
roam the fields and run around. The most charitable thing I can
say about the whole experience is that for nine months it took me
out of the population I might be infecting. It was a holding area
rather than an area addressed to ongoing treatments. I found it a
very unpleasant experience. After nine months when it was
perfectly obvious that I wasn't making any progress health wise
to my mother and that I was doing things she would never have
approved of, like running around all hours of the night, she
decided to take me home.

I stayed home. Between ten and one half and eleven years
(of age) my condition was worsening. I could not go back to
school. I had a communicable disease and they kept records.
They said I would have to go away immediately, and I did. They
sent me away to St Mary's which had just then opened in
Phoenix Park, because my condition was particularly bad. (There
was no) provision for the fact that I was quite young being put
with all adults many of whom were chronically and terminally
ill. There was no children's ward. I was in the ward with adults.
So, from that time on, that's the point that I can consciously
remember saying "Nobody else is going to take care of my life,
so I'm going to do it." And so I did. I was probably eight when
all this began. I was ten or eleven by the time I hit St Mary's. I
wasn't given a chance at some kind of education. They were
expecting me to die and there wasn't any point to it.

At the time I was eleven years old I came to the conclusion

that the doctors thought that I was already either physically dead or brain dead beacuse they always talked about me as if I didn't understand what they said. I began to have a very strong sense of class consciousness at that time. I was clearly aware that they thought I was a stupid inner city kid who didn't know anything. What they didn't know is that everything they wrote down on my chart, I took the chart later and read it. I knew exactly what they were talking about. I didn't pretend to anybody that I knew what was going on.

Whatever small amount of radio there was we had to pay for, but my mother couldn't afford it. Books were always the answer, the intellectual stimulus. They had a library. I read everything in the library. I was at St Mary's three and a half years. They did all kinds of experimental surgery. I was about fourteen and I made the decision myself that I was going to have the operation. It involved stripping the lining off the lung that was infected. They had to remove two ribs, which was very painful. It was the first time I was very distressed, because I realised what it was like to die of TB, not being able to breathe. I had oxygen for several days. It was a frightening experience. Almost like I had two sets of things going for me. There was the kid who was very frightened, and the other one who had grown up five years ago and said "This is another thing that is going to have to be dealt with."

I suspect that I didn't oblige them by dying off. My mother had been trudging up to this hospital for all these years and it was a great hardship on her. The doctors felt that the disease had been contained at that point, that I wasn't a danger to other people. But a doctor said within my presence "She probably won't last much beyond twenty." I think they thought that TB affects your ears and your head and everything and I resented it terribly. I thought "We'll just see about that."

I came home (when) I was fourteen or fifteen. There was no talk about me going to school because at that stage secondary school was not part of an inner city kid's agenda. I just continued to read at home. I didn't go out a lot. It took me a while to adjust to the social situation I was in. To even mix with people of my own age because I felt so much more mature. I felt like an old person. I actually stayed at home for three years. My mother worked, so I began to pick up the things in the house that she couldn't do, the housework. I took on little bits and pieces. I began to realise that I wasn't nearly the weakling that everybody said I was. And at about seventeen I asked my mother if she wouldn't pay for me to go to secretarial college, because I wanted to go to work. Now I wasn't sure that she begrudged the money, but I'm also quite certain that being the good Irish woman that she was and having the kind of respect for doctors' opinions that the Irish women did, she didn't really see the point of investing money in someone who was going to croak it in three years. Anyway, I decided, I told her that I would give it back in a year.

I did go to secretarial college and I did very well. I stayed on for another year. I went to work at the college. In the second year my mother was really pleased. Now they were paying me as well for secretarial assistance. So, I was no longer a financial burden on her. I think she was very proud of the fact that I'd actually gotten up and done this. Then one summer I went to London for two weeks and loved it. I came back and gave notice where I was working and went to London. I had a sister there. I got jobs galore. All of a sudden I realised "I am a viable human being." I did that for two years, got more and more confident as I got better and better jobs. Then I decided I hadn't given Dublin enough of a shot and I came back.

I was twenty two, twenty three, somewhere in there. I rattled around Dublin going from job to job, getting better jobs. I was secretary to the company which now runs Superquinn. I worked for Quinn's father. He ran a holiday camp called "Red Island." My lack of formal education didn't seem to interfere in any way with my ability to hold down a job. Finally, I joined the Irish Youth Hostelling Association. At this stage I'd long gone past my deadline for croaking. I started hiking and climbing and biking, all of the things that "delicate" people are not supposed to do. My mother got really upset and I said "look, whatever is left to me, I want to enjoy it. I want to do things like normal people" So I walked and biked and hiked all around Ireland, England, Scotland and Wales and I decided to conquer another continent. So, I decided to come to America.

None of the perceptions I had about America were true. Well, that everyone was a real blowhard. You had this funny idea about Americans that they never worked, that they always had plenty of of money, that they always seemed to be on vacation. They always had plenty of money, and they had no economic problems. And the working class in America just simply weren't visible to Europeans. Partly because when I was growing up in Dublin, the Americans we saw were the Americans who came after the War. They were older with more money.

I had not a single person (in America), but I really had a plan. It wasn't just a question of going to America, I wanted to go to Boston and San Francisco and then to Australia. Boston was the nearest, as simple as that. It was the easiest to get to. I loved Dublin. I loved the city of Dublin, its architecture, the feel of Dublin. From everything that I had heard of Boston, it was closer to the ideal of the city as I saw Dublin. I saw a movie that Alfred Hitchcock made and it showed pictures of New England in the Fall and I thought "I'd like to see that."

I signed up as, the nicest word for it was 'governess', and that's what they called me, but I really was a sort of a housekeeper who took care of the kids for a family in Woods Hole (on Cape Cod). An interesting thing that happened in my house (in Dublin) was an aunt of mine, who like everybody else was surprised that I survived at all, but was even more surprised that I had gone on to get a "Good Job," a step up in the social scale from where my mother and father would have expected me to work, both of them having come from working class families - my aunt was appalled that I was going to work as a housekeeper (in America). In fact, her words to my mother always stuck with me "How could you let her go and be a skivvy in somebody else's house, when she has the kind of background that she does?" To my mothers eternal credit she said "If I had her opportunity, I'd go too."

They sponsored me and I stayed with them for about a year. Then I decided I'd take a shot at working in Boston. The family were very interested in the fact that I didn't have a college education, and they thought I ought to have one. But I couldn't let other people make decisions for me. I came to Boston where a friend of my sister's happened to be a "Kelly Girl" (Temporary secretarial agency). She was going back to Ireland to get married. I had both an apartment and a job by the time I finally relocated in Boston. I wanted to be free and flexible. Right from the start I emigrated as a resident alien.

I was going to stay for a definite period. I think that's an escape valve, psychologically and unconsciously, that every person who leaves home, wherever it is, has to have. They have to have the notion that sooner or later they'll go back. It's almost like a security thing. I felt that at some point I would go back, but I always left it open-ended. But part of my psyche was shaped by the fact that my roots were so deluded from the very begining. It's taking charge of your own life from a very early age that makes the difference. I had to make decisions. I got more and more confident, but it gave me a sense of proving to myself that I could do it, overcoming seemingly absolutely impossible odds and obstacles. That shapes your whole life.

I came to Boston right after the time when it was considered to be very socially upscale to have a secretary who sounded almost British. A lot of people think my accent was a British accent. The people in Boston generally speaking only know the west of Ireland accent. Then somebody told me that if I went to work for Northeastern (University) there was the fringe benefit of free tuition. I went to work at the Dean of College of Business, and started taking courses, but got sick again. TB came back. My whole lung collapsed, it just couldn't withstand all the scarring that had healed over. I was thirteen years over my deadline for croaking. I was alone in my apartment and I started to haemorrhage very badly and I decided, this won't go away. This one I have to do something about. I was pumping out all this blood, but this was very old hack for me. The suggestion was made at Brigham and Women's (Hospital) that I should go home. I really felt there isn't anything they can do for me in Ireland that they can't do here. And if I went home I wouldn't have any insurance. They operated in December and I had my left lung taken out. Then I came home (to the apartment) on Christmas Day.

I was living in Mission Hill. I came home and I wasn't doing too well with the left arm because of course they had to do a lot of cutting, a lot of messy stuff. I had a wonderful Irish landlady who was very good to me. I decided that I probably would do well if I went off somewhere on a cruise. So I did. Three weeks later I took off by myself on a cruise to the Bahamas. My Irish landlady at that point said she was going to call my doctor to see if they took my brain out instead of my lung, because she thought I was absolutely mad.

I went on the cruise and came back and worked a lighter schedule. I was promoted from secretary to the Dean of the College of Business to secretary of the Office of the Executive Administrator and one of the Executive Administrators was my husband, who is the President (in 1988- now retired).

Chapter Six
The New Wave
The 1980s

Exiles

Those were the seedlings we sowed
pricked and primed
against the rock of poverty.
We have put names on their children
The children
of Gurley Flynn and Mother Jones
Oh your america.

Tumbletown and dead river valley
famine-forced they crowded the canals
from the Bog of Allen to Idaho,
crossed the Atlantic
in the stench of homelessness.

Now Bridie don't forget to say your prayers

Mother get me a bride
from out the four green fields
(my fields).

Mean fields.

Some got the lace
others fell like stones
uselessly

And ... to hell with the broken fingers
cooking fat at night
by candle quiver
We'll show you who the boss is
(a nickel a day, make hay make hay)
you Irish bitches ...

Now Bridie keep your legs crossed
and the rosary between your toes

Give me your fat.

But they rose ... rose ...
like bonfires on a mountain
every mansheila of them
rose against the whips
broke files, made unions.
It was a slow going
a slow coming.

Dear Bridie I received the dollars
your father's taken ill
I got shoes for Peadar
and Kathleen
I'll put the rest by
Pray for me

Why are we waiting
get me the DC.9
New York, New World
New suitcase, transit visa

Dear Uncle Tom get me a husband
and a Green card
And I'll never leave
your america

My Green Card -

Mean Card.

This is your pilot
Pointing Pilot
Feathering down on Kennedy Airport

Oh america

I strike out now
in a skyscrape of desire
shivering for dollars

You mean I've come all the way from Clontarf
And there's no job?

Suffered under pointing pilot
Why does everyone sleep
in the subway?

Leland Bardwell

By the late 1960s in the wake of the Immigration and Nationality
Act 1965 (which eliminated preferential treatment for nations of
the western hemisphere), Irish immigration to America almost
petered out as more people from Asia, South and Central
America sought new beginnings in the "Land of Dollars." This
virtual cessation of movement happened in tandem with
improved economic fortunes in Ireland. Dr TK Whitaker's white
paper on Economic Development laid the foundation for the
First Programme for Economic Expansion in 1958. Ireland was
now taking stock; less introverted, the Irish began aggressively
seeking foreign investors and export markets. This reversal in
policy was directly linked to emigration:

> After 35 years of native government people are asking
> whether we can achieve an acceptable degree of
> economic progress. The common talk among parents in
> the towns, as well as in rural Ireland, is of their children
> having to emigrate as soon as their education is
> completed in order to secure a reasonable standard of
> living.
> Dr TK Whitaker

Further, this economic rebirth brought about modernization particularly in education and social services, areas that most affected women's daily lives.

Concrete external developments such as the Anglo-Irish Free Trade Agreement in 1965 and European Community membership in 1973, put a new face on Ireland's economic affairs. So attractive had conditions become that emigrants were returning home. From 1971-81 the net in-migration (ie returning emigrants) to the Republic of Ireland was 104,000 people - both single people and entire families who had previously settled in Britain and America.

This positive picture did not continue long. Although the numbers of net new jobs were increasing throughout the 1970s, so too was population and, as a consequence, by the early 1980s unemployment more than doubled from 88,000 or 7.6% in 1975, to 206,000 or 15.6% om 1983. A major 'push' factor had emerged again and this time movement became more difficult than before. Particularly hard hit were the under-25 age group who made up almost half the population and were too far removed from the required nuclear family ties in America to claim legal entry. The United States had by this time established strict immigration regulations and entry now became a game of deception and performance at the INS (Immigration Naturalisation Service) booth at New York, Boston, San Francisco, or later on Irish soil at Shannon.

Coupled with this hardship was the fact that the profile and situation of the 1980s emigrant differed somewhat from previous years - young, single, but most of all highly educated. Unlike those emigrants of the 1950s who by the 1960s had moved into the more skilled jobs and were less involved in domestic/manual work, this new group brought comparatively higher qualifications to fewer opportunities. For Irish women the 'push' back to the kitchens and the kettles, to babies and making bread was a severe blow, since for most of those educated through the 1960s and 1970s the promise of equality of opportunity (hard won by the feminist movement in Ireland) had been dangled at the end of the long rope of education and training. In reality, they were worse off than their foresisters, since most were now forced to live as illegal immigrants, under constant strain of being discovered by the INS and deported.

Irish people continue to come to the USA and it is estimated that 150,000 emigrants have arrived since the start of the 1980s. It is difficult to put exact figures on the proportion of women to men since this vulnerable population cannot easily be tabulated. However, it is clear that a market exists with a high demand for nannies and home help, areas of employment traditionally associated with Irish women. Their vulnerable position leaves them open to abuse as employers seek to take advantage of child minders and cleaners whom they know to be working illegally. Fearing deportation, they often remain quiet when abuses in employment occur. Fearing loss of their men to drink or "freer" American women, these new '80s Irish women often enter live-in relationships sooner than they would at home, or seek American men to marry to alleviate their undocumented distress, and acquire a "green card."

However, recent legislation has been enacted in an attempt to alleviate the position of undocumented emigrants. The 'Donnelly visas' - allocated 45,000 permanent work permits on a first-come- first-served lottery system for people from Western Europe affected by the 1965 legislation. A surprisingly high percentage of these have gone to Irish people. The more recent 'Berman' visas raised many hopes of legalisation of the 'new' Irish illegals, but few have been awarded to Irish people.

Following a path carved out by earlier movers, these 1980s women leave an Ireland undergoing severe economic hardship despite all the good omens of the 1960s. And they also leave a country which has recently introduced legislation even more repressive towards women. The difficult years of the 1981-1983 anti-abortion campaign left what Nell McCafferty called an "unwomanly legacy." The Eighth Amendment to the Constitution read: "The State acknowledges the right to life of the unborn, and, with due regard to the equal right to life of the mother, guarantees in its laws to respect, and as far as practicable by its laws to defend and vindicate that right." The Constitutional Amendment ensured that the flow of thousands of Irish women leaving the country annually for abortions in England would continue. The Republic underwent extreme division as the Amendment was hotly debated in the media and in churches across the nation. Shortly after the Amendment was passed the

Society for the Protection of the Unborn Child launched another successful campaign and so prevented any information on abortion being dissiminated in Ireland.

The Referendum of 1986, unsuccessful and rushed, was called to seek the abolition of the Constitutional prohibition on divorce. Many women whose whole life and career was marriage were afraid to vote for the abolition of the clause because it was unclear what kind of legislation the Dáil would seek to introduce once they were given the power to leglislate on divorce. TD (Dáil member) Alice Glenn compared women voting for this Referendum to "turkeys voting for Christmas." At the centre of this debate was the question of property and the perception that the alternative to many a failed, abusive, painful marriage was poverty for women and children. Without the support of State childcare after divorce, no woman could possibly afford to raise chilren alone, work inside and outside the home and begin life afresh. Women rightfully understood that although the State lauded the family and purported to love each and every foetus, the reality was that the concrete supports needed by women to ensure a proper and fair life for children outside of unhappy or abusive marriages did not exist.

Three other cases brought to the attention of Irish women during the decade of the 1980s further signalled and reinforced the mysogynist message of Irish society. The 'Kerry Babies Inquiry' was set up to investigate the connection of Joanne Hayes to a baby found washed ashore on the Kerry coast. The Inquiry, instead of focusing on the issues relating to the murder, addressed all its attention to Joanne's relationship with a married man, her sexual history and the death of her own infant at home.[27] Anne Lovett, a young teenager, and her newborn infant were found dead by a grotto to the Virgin Mary in the small town of Granard in County Longford. This young woman could find no one within this family-oriented nation to listen to her calls for help. Eileen Flynn, a teacher, was sacked from her job because of her relationship with a married man.

Though the economic situation was indeed bleak and unemployment reached record highs, the atmosphere created by this series of events must also have had a bearing on women's decision to leave Ireland.

Despite these difficulties many emigrants come to America and triumph in their own ways. Representing the tales of the undocumented are LL from Leitrim, MM from Tipperary, and RR from Cork, and the documented Rena Cody from Dublin, Teresa O'Hara from Galway and Máire Ní Bhranlaigh from Sligo. Their voices are included to illustrate not only how certain factors remain a constant in the emigration process (hope, loss, grief, dependency, networks, support), but also how the strength of women shines through. More and more Irish women in the USA do not expect their men to look after them. The concept of self-reliance has been transmitted through the generations of daughters. They, like their foresisters, have power, often used in subtle ways and the verbal dimension to their actions must be presented.

LL

LL comes from Ballinamore, a small village in County Leitrim. After completing secondary school, she moved to Dublin to work in the Civil Service, returning each weekend to Ballinamore. She got leave of absence from her job in 1985, came to America and has remained here ever since.

She took the leave of absence to pacify her parents who were very much opposed to her move. Though not necessarily forced to emigrate because of unemployment as many of the "New Irish" are, LL was nonetheless discontent with her job and saw no prospects for advancement for herself as a woman in a system based on seniority alone. Her story tells us of the kinds of strategies used to survive and work as an undocumented woman, highlighting some of the unchanging aspects of life as an emigrant. However, LL's story predates the new Immigration regulation which requires that employers request proof of eligibility before work begins.

I lived in the country, about five miles outside the town, on a farm. I've one brother and three sisters. But after I left school I wasn't around Ballinamore that much, I would just return at the weekend. About ninety per cent of the young people there are working in Dublin or abroad.

At Curragh Races, Boston 1989
Photograph: Caitríona Cooke

I was a Clerical Officer in the Civil Service. I wasn't happy
in my job. I got no satisfaction out of it. It was a secure job and it
was what everybody calls a good job, but to me it wasn't a good
job. I really wanted to come to this country when I was twenty,
but my father wouldn't let me come. I'd heard about it from
relatives and I'd heard about it from friends of mine that come
out here young, like nineteen, eighteen. I know a lot of people
that came out with nothing and nothing to return to. But I've
played it well on both sides, because I held on - only for my
family I wouldn't have held on so long. I got leave and came to
America.

I was in the Civil Service three and a half years. I was one of
the last people into my Department. Promotion wasn't on merit -
to get promotion in that kind of job there are exams you can do,
but it's like twenty positions for a couple of hundred people. I
felt there was no way I could stick twenty years until I got to the
top.

I flew into New York and I met my friends, a neighbour
from home and the first thing she said to me was "Are you not
excited that you're in the biggest city in the world?" I looked
around me. I wasn't overwhelmed by that city at all. I was more
excited about coming to Boston. I felt more at home in Boston.

When I arrived in Boston it was just like a bigger version of
Dublin. I felt so comfortable. Boston was just my city. I have
second cousins here. I stayed with them for two weeks and then I
got a live-in job minding a baby, two months old. I stayed in that
job for six months. I got an apartment with my brother and I
started cleaning. I was waitressing, then (I worked as) a cook in
an Irish bar in Brighton. I decided this wasn't the type of work I
wanted to do.

I didn't expect to be able to do what I wanted to do here. I
thought I was limited to the things you know about in Ireland -
when you don't have a green card or working papers you're
limited to waitressing, babysitting or minding old people or
children. That's what I was led to believe, that was all you can do
in America when you're not legal. I think there's a lot more you
can do if you're legal or not. If you fight hard enough for it and if
you work your way around it, there are things you can do. I
know it takes a lot of gall, but if you're so depressed with your
job, you're bound to find a way out if you get up and go.

So, I hunted for a job, something I might like. I took papers
and I searched through them for a whole two weeks and I finally

came to the conclusion, having read all the ads, that there were a
lot of dental assistants needed in this country. I applied for three
jobs and went for three interviews. All of them wanted me. I
took the one on Beacon Street, with Dr S. I told them I had
experience of about three months working with a dentist at
home. I never worked as a dental assistant, but in order to get
what I wanted to get I had to lie. I didn't mind lying at the time
because I was desperate for the job. I just didn't like what I was
doing, plus the fact that I wasn't making enough money. Also, I
like to have something steady, because you're going to have your
rent every month, and your bills, and I think it's important to
have a job where you know what you're getting every week. I
wanted something stable, more secure than waitressing.

The dentist was giving me about three hundred and eleven
before tax, so I was coming out with two fifty. Plus the fact that I
kept some of my cleaning jobs for Saturdays, which meant that I
had that little bit extra money.

Nobody asked me for any documentation. His accountant
asked me over the phone for my social security number for tax
reasons, and I had a made-up number. I gave him the number
and I've never had a problem.

I pay taxes every week. I'm not living off anybody. I'm not
living off the government. I'm here willing to work, willing to
pay my taxes and I only wish to God that they'd make more of us
legal. I didn't tell them much about my status at work. I don't like
to tell too many people how I stand. There are one or two that I
can trust, but I don't put my faith in trusting everybody. I had
come on a visitor's visa, and I'm still here.

When my dentist retired I was automatically interviewed by
a cousin of his. I went to work for him. He couldn't wait for me
to start, so he held out for three months until I finished my other
job. I was well recommended. I'm a fairly good time keeper and
I'm rarely sick.

When the new office manageress asked me if I had any
papers to show that I was legally bound (entitled) to work in this
country my first reaction was "What am I going to do now?" So I
acted kind of quickly and said I'd returned my working papers to
Ireland to have them extended. After two months she asked for
the papers again. So, I put a date on when I'd have to go home,
because there was another job coming up minding old people. A
friend of mine referred me to this agency. I tested out the job and
it nearly drove me insane. I think it's more important to have less

money and better health, than to have yourself going crazy for the sake of a few dollars.

I told them at the dentist's office that I'd have to go to Ireland because of my papers. He asked if there was anything he could do and he would. The office manageress said "We'll keep you as long as we can. We'll be willing to back you." If I thought there was any way around this problem, doing an exam even, I'd do it. It's the kind of work I love to do and I'm not going to drop it that easy just for the sake of a paper. I hope he will sponsor me. Right now I'm considering talking to a lawyer. He'll obviously have to be an immigration lawyer.

I'd think about going home twice before I'd go. I'd love to be able to go home free and easy and come back. It's no big problem going home, it's a big problem coming back.

My ambition is to return to Ireland some day. I'd like to have my own business in about five years time. If it's more than five I'll wait until it's time to go. I always had it in my mind, but my wages in Ireland would never allow me to do so. If I was to get married and have a family, I'd like to rear them in Ireland. As much as this country offers people, and I think it's a great country and everything, but I would rather have my family in Ireland. I think it's a safer country and a nicer country for kids to be brought up in. I certainly wouldn't like to get old in this country. Elderly people are very lost and alone here.

I would like to think I could return and be able to come back here, maybe with an amnesty or a green card, and be able to come and go. It would be nice.

RR

RR is a Cork woman, the youngest of a family of five. She worked in England before coming to the USA in 1987. She has just completed a year's work as a nanny/housekeeper for a wealthy family in Milton, Massachusetts. Most young Irish women do work of a similar nature, certainly most of the undocumented or "illegals" of the 1980s. Of particular concern is the fact that many of these young women are open to abuse because of their vulnerable position with immigration and also since most are live-in help, thus isolated from relatives or friends. Long hours and poor wages are common complaints.

However, RR was lucky. Her family reside in a wealthy suburb of Boston, and she has the use of a car at all times. She has found that rather than confining her, the responsibility of being in charge of an entire household and two small children has given her a new self-confidence to do things she always wanted to do eg quilting. Her quilts are unique pieces of artwork, and reflect South American colour schemes with Irish motifs. Uncertain of her future, she cannot plan ahead since she is constantly trying to find ways of legalising her position. Her ultimate aim is to return to Ireland and start her own business.

I arrived in Boston from London in May of 1987. Siobhán, a friend of mine was already married here in Boston and she was on to me to come out. At the time I had no real commitment to London, so I decided to come.

I went to the local national school, St Catherine's and then St Angela's in Cork. From there I went to the NIHE in Limerick (now University of Limerick), but didn't complete the course. It was during the time of unrest there and it didn't suit me. In London I did secretarial work and from there got a job in the West Indies for a year.

I visited my brother, a priest in South America, came back and tried to settle in Cork. I made a big effort; got involved in things, but I found the community was too small, too many of the same people everywhere. I went back to London and then on to Boston. I was ripe; I was in the situation that I wanted to go.

Siobhán had told me that because of the new legislation it probably would be quite difficult to find work, but I was in the situation where I wanted to try it and see. I came and applied for jobs. They wanted either proof of being born in America, or a working visa. At that stage I was quite disillusioned - the whole thing about living a lie - I felt I couldn't do it.

I met another girl I had known vaguely in Cork who was working as a nanny. Both she and another girl from Cork had set themselves up as nannies. They were pleased with the jobs; their situation was very good. The following Sunday I got the *Sunday Globe* and started ringing around. I knew what I was looking for - if I was minding a child, I wanted to mind it while the mother was out. I did not want the situation where I was a mother's helper.

I spoke with CS (present employer). She and her husband worked from seven in the morning to seven in the evening. They wanted somebody to come in and basically raise/mind the children and run the house. She had a nanny at the time from Scotland, so I reckoned at that stage she knew the situation about work permits. She never asked did I have a visa to work here.

I told her I reckoned I should get two hundred dollars a week. She insisted I have health insurance - I would have to pay half. The position I'm in right now I'm enjoying it. I do more with my time - things I've always wanted, talked about doing. I've started quilting, I go swimming, go to aerobics. I enjoy the time I have for myself right now.

I would like to think that after this experience I would be in a position where I could generate a business myself - be it quilting, teaching quilting, something like that (in Ireland). To set me up and help me, I send cash home to my bank account because I don't have a bank account here.

I've met another girl from Cork who minds a child and through the swimming at the "Y" I've met girls who are nannies, not necessarily Irish. I don't go to the Irish bars, but I will go to an Irish concert. I'm in America and don't want to hang out in Irish bars.

I get great job satisfaction and I don't have any stress. It's very rewarding, but then again I work for very nice people.

I like to think I'll go home to Ireland eventually. I feel more confident now. When I was a secretary I always felt I was never really happy.

When I left school fourteen years ago very few people were emigrating (1974). If anything you went to London for a few years' experience and then came back and set up at home. Everybody is leaving, even people with jobs because all their friends have left, which is difficult.

I will just have to wait and see what my opportunity will be. If I got an opportunity to go home, I would go, but then again if I got the opportunity to stay, I'd stay. I'm not saying. I don't know. I never do know and I'll be thirty two in June (1988).

Leena Deevy

Leena Deevy, who hails from Laois, had lived and worked some twenty five years in Ballymun flats in Dublin. She left school at seventeen and trained to be a nurse in Wales. She joined the Sisters of the Assumption and in 1987 she came to the USA to rest and during her stay applied to the Harvard School of Education for a place on their Masters in Education Programme. She will graduate in the summer of 1990.

I was born in the middle of the bog, a place called Cretty Ard, near the Castlecomer border. My father was in this country (USA) when he was about nineteen or twenty; spent thirteen years here. Thirteen years driving buses in New York. His family was in the Civil War, so politics in our house were very important and when there was an election we didn't talk to anybody who was in Fine Gael. You were friends with them all the rest of the year, but once the elections came up you didn't talk with them until they were over. My father and Oliver J Flanagan were always fighting.

There were seven of us on a farm. My father came from a poor family. My father's father married three times and my father married three times. He went to America and came back much more what I'd call a worker with a Protestant ethic. He bought this little farm. He'd always say things like "If people worked half as hard as they did in America, there wouldn't be all the poverty." He was quite judgemental. He'd get up at five in the morning and be home from the creamery at six - a workaholic. So, he wouldn't have integrated well into the local (community). The only time he'd go out was to political meetings.

I was the second youngest. My mother was the local nurse. Up at the crack of dawn, non stop we worked. My father believed in education, but there was always too much work to do to read anything. Work non stop, before you went to school, and when you came home from school and every other time as well. I had mixed school until twelve, protestants and catholics. There was a lot of protestants lived in our neighbourhood. Then I went to a convent school in Carlow. At eighteen I went nursing to North Wales. I knew a girl who was there.

When we were at school we had two streams, A and B. If you were bright you went to University and if you were dull you either did a secretarial course or went nursing - and there were finances as well. I probably would have preferred social work at that stage, but I was interested in helping people and there was a tradition, my mother was a nurse. There was also the fact that I didn't think I'd have the grades to get into University. It wasn't acceptable then for girls to go to Uni either, out in the country it was more acceptable that you go more into nursing or into the convent or things like that.

I was in Wales four years. Then I came back to Holles Street (Maternity Hospital). I was there for a year, then I joined up (the Little Sisters of the Assumption). I was young and enthusiastic. I was basically interested in working with people and at that stage my religion would have meant an awful lot to me. I wanted to go to South America. I didn't want to go into an institution. I didn't particularly like nuns. In fact I hated nuns at that stage. I wanted to do some of the stuff that my mother used to be doing when she used to be going into families. I always had a very strong social conscience. I felt that poor people were very badly treated. Our particular group (Little Sisters) started to work where there's mothers rearing children or where a mother is sick and there was nobody to look after the children.

I always was very incensed with and ambivalent about the church, about the institutional side of the church. I liked my mother's religion and I hated my father's religion. My father's was preaching. This is why I very seldom talk about religion or that side of my life. I wasn't going to join a group to either convert anybody or preach to anybody. I wanted to be more of a friend to people. The side of religion that I saw in my father and in the institutional side at home was to do with preaching. I decided one time I would never talk about religion or why I was doing what I was doing, just do it. I started working in Ballyfermot first, then Finglas and then Ballymun (Dublin suburbs). I discovered there were a lot of things I enjoyed doing there (in Ballymun). So, I changed myself as well. South America didn't have the same attraction for me. I just got so absorbed in where I was. I always like working with....and I don't like the term "working class." I never felt comfortable in upper class or middle class circles. I used to get very angry when people used say to me "Aren't you great to be working in Ballymun." I used to think that was an awful insult.

There were three of us there in the seventies. I started out originally doing nursing. I was interested in family planning. So, I started doing family planning. I mainly did natural methods and advice on other methods. If people wanted to buy some contraceptives, I'd give them advice. I got plenty of flack over it. I was in an office which we got shoved out of because somebody didn't like me doing family planning. I also felt there was a need for a more comprehensive service. I couldn't provide that within my scope. So, I moved out of that and I was doing a lot of social work at the time with families who were at risk. Then I was involved in youth groups. When I moved into Ballymun I had no role as a nurse, so I started to work around whatever the needs were, responding to it and adapting to whatever needed to be done.

I got very interested in Paulo Freire's method of working with people. You work with people to sort out their problems - group people together and people themselves come up with their needs and how they want to respond to their own needs. So, basically I started to train people to run their own projects. Originally I was a very hard worker and had lots of energy and creativity and found that a better way of working was to work with people rather than for people. So, I'd have changed drastically over a few years.

I'd spend a lot more time chatting with people. Like one of my beliefs is that women have an awful lot of talent. I saw women having little or no confidence and not feeling they could do much themselves. But I knew that they had an awful lot of innate ability. I felt that my role at that stage was to create opportunity for them to get in touch with that ability, and where they could get training. Now, I mightn't be the one to do the training, but I saw myself more as a link between people in Ballymun and people I knew had ability and training. At that stage I was also good at getting things done for nothing. I can't get it done over here at all. I'd ring up people and never dream of offering to pay them or anything - courses on assertiveness or child development.

I worked a lot with different groups; tenant's groups, community drugs project, whatever groups were there. The Health Board asked would I set up a Home Help Service. I really didn't want to take the job on. It was a push. It had to do with finances. I was in a bind. I wasn't working for anybody in particular, I was freelancing. I was a nurse and I wasn't nursing. I wasn't a qualified social worker and I was doing lots of in-depth work with families. I was doing family planning and I was a nun. I was doing youth groups and I wasn't a team leader.

I used to find half my time in meetings apologising for my existence. I also knew there was a stage in Dublin where there was a lot of suspicion of nuns. A lot of people didn't like nuns. They thought I had a hidden agenda because I was a nun. I felt much less comfortable with the institutional side of the church, yet I was linked to that. At one stage I was running a play group and every morning I used to go over there was glue in the door because there was a group who didn't agree with me running the play group because I was a nun. People would say that I was colluding with the system. That stage would have been difficult for me, but I am a survivor. A lot of people of the "Left," whatever Left is, would have been very suspicious of me. But I know now they have a huge respect for me.

Eventually, I started off the Home Help thing (Health Board Project) which I hated doing because the money was very small, women were paid very badly as home helps, which they still are. My job was to get women and train them to put them into work with families or elderly who needed home help in Ballymun and wider Santry. I decided maybe we can use Paulo Freire's method with this. We started training all the home helps. I used the situation to do assertivness training and personal development and we negotiated money from ANCO for them. So, by the time I was leaving all the home helps were trained and we had a team of home helps running the service. We did peer group supervision and developed a Home Aid Service. I'd say the home help service in Ballymun is the best run in the country, the best run in Europe.

I was all the time fighting in a new kind of role, a new battle, a new cause. Ploughing new ground all the time, bringing up all these ideas. We ran, Hugh Docherty and I, a six month leadership programme, negotiated funding with ANCO; twenty leaders, people who were on tenantss association or in the co-ops, all kinds of groups. There's three parishes in the area and there are people from the Left and the Right and the middle and the east, and men and women, younger and older, we got them all together. Part of the reasoning behind it was that I felt that poor people can do themselves a lot of damage by internal conflicts. Now there's a job centre and a credit union and all kinds of things. We also started return to work courses for women and they were the last thing before I came away. That was formulated into a training agency. They're running leadership training courses out in Tallaght now from Ballymun.

I was a total wreck when I came here because I'd worked extremely hard. I was a workaholic basically. That's why I never had time to write. I did a lot of reflecting. One of the things that was significant was accepting the stand I took on the divorce issue. I would have made a lot of friends and a lot of enemies on that. My postition was that we should have a separate church and state and that divorce should be there for people who want it. So, I was interviewed in *The Irish Times* as the alternative church view. After the divorce referendum a lot of people who would have a certain amount of unease about where I stood knew after that. It was strange the reaction of people. Some told me I was damned to hell. One woman rang me and told me I was in mortal sin. But I didn't worry about it. I had consciously decided in Ballymun I wouldn't ever go on television unless I absolutely had to. I felt it was much more important to encourage people from the area to do the talking. But I thought that this was one time that was very important for somebody within the church to make an alternative statement.

I was wrecked and needed distance. I was coming on a holiday to America. I didn't want to face the fact that I was leaving Ballymun because my life was Ballymun. I lived it and loved it, ate and slept it. I liked the people there. There was an honesty and I felt there was no trying to be something. Everybody had struggles and nobody was putting on any great show for anybody else. I had vaguely in the back of my mind to apply to Harvard but thought "if it's meant to be, I'll get in." I applied and I got in. That was it. I came wanting to get away from problems.

I've enjoyed it. I've been glad to be away from Ireland. I like the international flavor of the programme. I found it extremely difficult coming into an academic setting and still do. I go into the depths of depression over it. I suppose I'm kind of pleased I'm managing ok and I've got on well so far. I'm not sticking out like a sore thumb. Being at Harvard has affirmed me, has hit all my deepest insecurities and fears.

Being a nun, people think you're a bit off the wall in a narrow, rigid way. You couldn't be normal not having sexual relationships. It's difficult to get people to accept me as a person. I tend to be either loved or hated. It's difficult to be totally free in oneself when you belong to a specific group and I am because people have you, have decided what type of person I am.

American life to me depends on what side of America you look at. There are some parts of American life that I really like. I like the open society, the mixture of people. What I don't like is the division between the rich and the poor. One of the things I find most difficult is the numbers of homeless people here in

Boston. I pass them every morning and I was thinking I was
back in Ireland, except there is a lot more money in this country.
I don't like how ethnic groups, black people or native American
people are treated. I came here with a prejudice against
Americans because I didn't agree with policy in Nicaragua and
Central America and I would have a strong aversion to Reagan
and his politics. I was involved in marches when Reagan was in
Ireland. So, I came here with anti-American feeling, but I also
came here very open, aware that with the size of the country
you'd meet all kinds of people.

I might end up in Belfast. I'd be interested in working with
protestants and catholics in Belfast. We've (the order) a place
near to the Flats (Divis Flats).

Teresa O'Hara

Teresa was actually born in New York. Her parents had
emigrated in the 1950s and returned to Galway when Teresa was
two years old. They went back and forth three more times in the
space of three years before eventually settling in Ireland. After a
degree in social work Teresa went to the London School of
Economics to study for her Masters in health care policy.
However, she found no market for her skills. She has emerged as
a significant leader within the Irish Immigration Reform
Movement, a movement founded by Irish immigrants.

My mother is from Mayo and my father is from Leitrim.
Both of them emigrated in the fifties and got married
there. My father always had a great desire to go back and live in
Ireland. My mother had also, but she was a little more practical.
There were six kids in the family at this time.

We lived on 85th Street on the East Side. There were
extended vacations where we were deciding whether we were
going to stay or if it was just a vacation. I did go back and forth a
few times.

When I was about four my memory of the place was that it
was so green and so much more free. We used to play on the
streets of Manhattan. My parents in one of their moods had
bought a house in Galway. I was the fourth child and there were
two more after me. That was part of the reason for moving back
to America, because they had the house and the mortgage. My

parents didn't want to split up. So, they decided if he had to move to get work, we'd all move. I know that the last move when we finally got settled (in Galway) was in 1972. I know it wasn't good so much movement especially for young kids.

In 1972 I was eight. I lived in Merlin Park, just a little suburb outside Galway. It wasn't unusual for kids to be coming back from America. I was happy there. In a sense I never remember missing a lot about America. I went to national school, then to the Mercy convent. Then after that I went to University College, Dublin. I a did Social Science degree. It was something that it was impossible to get a job at in Ireland. I stayed in Ireland for about six months but found it really difficult to get work. Basically the sort of work I was doing was shop work, to make some money. I started thinking about graduate school.

I was interested in some kind of social planning or health administration. In some senses my reasons for looking in that area was because I felt they were areas where people were needed at home. Then I would get a job in Ireland if I had a more definite, more specific qualification. I felt there weren't people qualified in terms of heath planning. I picked the course in London because I figured it would give me a better mix in terms of the National Health Service and the kind of health system in Ireland. Before I went to England I needed to make money for the fees, so I came to New York first in March of 1986.

I was just doing general administrative assistant. I stayed until August of that year. I enjoyed it. I knew it wasn't long term, but I knew from being there that it wasn't a place I wanted to live. I had a sister there and not only that, I had a lot of friends that had emigrated.

The London School of Economics course was a Masters in Health Planning and Financing geared to developing countries and so a lot of my class were from Asia or South America or places like that. I felt I was at home with a lot of these people more than I did with a lot of English people. I didn't know any Irish people at all in London.

While I was on the course I made arrangements with the Western Health Board (in Ireland) to attend their monthly meetings. I had contacts with people in the Department of Health. I had practically a job set up for myself and then in March of that year, with the budget, they put an embargo on employing people in the Civil Service. I didn't feel too bitter at the time because I knew what the government was doing just had to be done. I really did feel there were too many people in the Civil Service. I was beginning to feel disheartened that because they had to cut back they couldn't see that people were willing to use their qualifications to help make the situation a better one. But they hadn't got the chance. I said I'd work voluntarily and they said they had their own people already for it.

I couldn't stay in Ireland without a source of income and I couldn't stay and go on the dole and hope a job would just turn up in six months time. I really hadn't much choice but to go somewhere else and I didn't pick England as a first choice because I had been there and I knew that most of my friends in my network were not English. I had been to America before and because I was a citizen I knew it would be easy for me to get a job. I felt that was my only option at the moment in 1987.

Boston was the best place for me to go to get work experience. There were a lot of hospitals here and people sort of termed it the medical capital of the United States. I didn't know anyone in Boston. I stayed with a distant relative of my boyfriend's. She was spinster. I was very careful when I was living with her to make sure that I knew my place, but she just couldn't cope with the fact that I was this young, educated person. She couldn't understand when I was turning down jobs paying fifteen and sixteen thousand dollars because they weren't the type of work I wanted to do. She had worked here in the same job for twenty years. Probably she resented the fact that somebody like me was coming along and had everything ahead of me. She was just as intelligent and could have had the same opportunities if things had worked out different for her. I think that caused her a lot of bitterness. I would go to Irish history lectures and she'd just make comments like "you'd think you'd know enough about that from home." It just didn't work out and in the end I met this girl doing temp work and she offered to put me up.

My aunt, my mother's sister, lives in Maynard (outside of Boston). Her husband is from Galway and all of his brothers and sisters are here. Basically the whole family emigrated. Even though they visit Ireland every year they don't want it to get better, because they're never going to go back there and they'd rather see it the way it has been left. They've toned down a lot more, seeing as a lot of their nieces and nephews are coming over.

Margaret Carlson (1920s) with her daughter
and granddaughter, 1989
Photograph: Caitríona Cooke

I was very lonely when I came here first because I was saying I was making a definite move - two years or whatever. Two years seemed like a long stretch, it wasn't by choice that I left. My whole plans up to then had been geared to staying at home and then all of a sudden all of that changed and I did feel that in some ways it was a situation I was forced into. I would have been happy to stay in Ireland, my main priority of going was to get work experience.

I really didn't know where to start here because the system is so different. It's not like the Department of Health making plans and policy. It took me a long time to get work and I did get very disillusioned with my qualifications. Eventually, I worked with a representative in the State House - John McDonagh. I figured that there is some kind of planning of health service at the State level and maybe this was a way of hooking into it. I had my loan (from studying in England) still at the back of my mind, so I started waitressing for about four months. After I finished that I went home to Ireland for a month.

It was the Christmas of 1988. When I was home I realised that things were getting a little bit better, but it still wasn't time to think about settling back there yet. I came back here and I was really positive about finding a job, something in health administration, to learn about the whole business of health care here. In America it's just a big business. I started looking for health care work. My first job was a research assistant in a project that was at Harvard School of Public Health. It was just a temporary job, working budgets, looking at health in developing countries. I knew it was temporary and I continued looking for work. Eventually, I got the job I'm in now. It's in Boston City Hospital, in Paediatrics.

They call me the grants manager. There's about thirty four to forty research grants. A lot of Paediactric AIDS and women that take drugs when they're pregnant. My job is to co-ordinate the system. It has given me an opportunity to see how a whole department is run here. Basically I set up the whole system of how they look at individual budgets and another system to integrate them with the main department. I feel that if I do stay in Boston for another few years I won't stay in that job. I'll look for something better. A lot depends on when I go home this Christmas. I'm going to try and meet with some people connected with business studies programmes in Ireland. If they feel I'm acceptable enough, I'll go back home for a Masters in

Business Studies - a programme that concentrates on planning and organizational studies. It's something that I feel eventually for work in Ireland will be a good qualification. Ireland being a society that is in change, a lot of organisational systems will have to change. I'd be very interested in looking at planning and adapting it to the changes that will have to take place. My main priority is to go back and work in Ireland. Getting a qualification from UCD (Master's In Business Administration) would give me the opportunity to look at the Irish and European systems, and make some contacts in an Irish setting for work afterwards.

I did feel I was privileged in a sense that with my green card, or American citizenship, I could come here and choose what work I wanted to do. I really felt for people that came here and maybe had career as a priority as well and would like to get work experience, but were unable to do so because they hadn't the proper documentation. I did get involved in different committees of the Irish Immigration Reform Movement, the Political Action Committee. I didn't become involved in the main committee until this year, January of 1989. I know the goals (of the IIRM) are very good and legitimate in terms of trying to work on legislation, but for me in someways it was a bit vague and not something I could put a lot into. At the end of last year they started developing the HOT LINE and trying to have more outreach to immigrants. I got involved developing the social aspects of the group just to be aware of the needs of the current members. What people wanted was ways of establishing friends. They wanted to feel that if they invested their time and turned up one week they were going to see these people again.

It was the women who did a lot of the groundwork, running around just making sure that the office functioned. In terms of the social thing, it didn't get a lot of support initially from the group. They couldn't see the connection between Irish immigrants and their needs and this organisation wasn't developing to match those needs. They were losing touch with the population they were trying to serve. They were forgetting that it wasn't just undocumented people were here, but a lot of 'Donnelly' people too. I felt that by offering services that the political reform could come along with that. When we incorporated some of the male people on the committee I wasn't sure what their agenda was - for genuine immigration reform or what. At other times I felt they just enjoyed the whole power trip of the whole organisation. It wasn't until we actually

incorporated at an annual general meeting that there was a kind
of reshuffle of the group and I began to feel a lot more powerful
and putting a lot more effort into it. I can make decisions as well
as the men on the group and I'm as well able to fight and stand
up for the rights of young Irish immigrants. It's just that I would
go about it in a different way.

The men, most of them are in labouring jobs and then with
women a lot of them are doing child care work or elderly care. I
felt more acutely for women than I did for men because some of
these guys would have done that work at home anyway. They
would have been carpenters or construction workers, and there's
not too many of them that have degrees. Maybe there are a few,
but I don't think it's the majority, in no sense. A lot of the women
- I really feel that they're wasted and that's a bigger injustice.
Men are tending to put down women more in some senses and I
think the whole dynamic with the IIRM was when we started
becoming more vocal it was like - it's just women, into the social
things, they'll be just as well off looking after the children. No
wonder they weren't promoting that side of it (social work,
outreach). They felt we were going to ruin their organisation.

We went to New York to visit the group there (headoffice of
the IIRM). I felt bad for most of the women that came with me.
We all went around and said what we did besides the IIRM.
Most of them did say childcare and elderly care. Then when it
came to me, involved with the grants, and straight away he was
saying "I have to send you such and such." I felt that
subconsciously, whether we realise it or not, it (the work an
immigrant women does) does affect men's image of women.
Things like that do make me feel bad because I do feel that there
is no reason why it should be that way. They should only be in
those jobs by choice, if they want to, not because they're
undocumented.

In terms of the IIRM, I try to get different people in actually
running the events. We're going to develop a whole lot more on
the social side of things, networking with other groups. (The
Emerald Isle Inc is now a sub company of the IIRM) We have a
radio show going now and I'd like to see more people getting
something out of it.

The majority talk about returning to Ireland eventually. It's
something amazing, very, very few talk about staying here
longterm. I do know a few people who do, people who have met
people over here and they're going to get married. Most people

have this vision of eventually settling back home, saving up the money for the time when they return to Ireland. I think things are changing a bit at home, but it does take having dynamic people who are going to get involved in changing the system. It won't be easy at first. You have to have a vision for the country or some sort of allegiance to go. I have this vision of Ireland at the moment that it doesn't have a young population, that they're all leaving. That's why I see the need for emigrants coming back. These are the people that can help change the country.

MM

MM is a talented young musician from Tipperary who emigrated to the USA in 1985. She had been married a year, was twenty years of age and five months pregnant. She and her husband could not meet the mortgage on their home in Limerick even though both worked.

In Boston she had her baby boy and shortly after that divorced her alcoholic husband. She sees the position of Irish women immigrants in America as worse than that of women in Ireland or those that came before them in earlier waves of emigration. Therefore, she stresses the need for unity amongst Irish women abroad.

Since this interview she has married an Irish-American and still lives in Dorchester, Boston.

My father owned a garage. There were ten in my family. They are all scattered - Australia, mostly England, Canada, two in Ireland. I'm the youngest.

I did the Leaving Cert (examination) and a Commercial course. I had been to a boarding school to get out of the small town mentality. I think my mother's idea was to go and see what it's really like when you come back. There were orchestras and choirs - I wanted to do a music degree, but I wanted to get out. I'd stagnated for a few years.

I got married at nineteen in Limerick. We bought a house and I worked, but there was a terrible financial strain. We couldn't get any stuff for the house. It was such a struggle. I was five months pregnant. He (husband) came over in November. He had a friend over here (who) said there was plenty of work. Two weeks later he went. We tried to arrange to sell, to rent the

house; eventually I came over on November 30th. We had
nothing. I didn't think I had the train fare to Boston. Immigration
at Boston was worse.

We stayed with his friend. I was five months pregnant and
no idea how I was going to have the child. I had nothing. There
was a huge panic on to save money for the four remaining
months of the pregnancy. Both of us worked. We saved and
lived on nothing. We went to a very low standard of living - not
living properly. It was almost skipping life.

I had made myself up a number and I went into a law firm,
got a job as a receptionist. About a year later I moved on before
the 1986 employer sanctions. I stayed at that job.

Then we got divorced. It was drink basically and I'd say that
will be the breaking up of a lot of marriages. There's a huge
problem over here. It's such a male oriented society. I'm not
majorly feminist, but I'm majorly people - I think there can be an
equalness between people that can balance out and doesn't
necessarily show up in who does what around the house.

The women at home are better off then the women over here.
In marriages here men are at a huge advantage. They're at double
and treble the wages. The financial reins are back securely in the
hands of men again. This is how women are down in the more
menial jobs. You don't have the status; you can't blame it all on
the men, that's what American legislation rules (do).

From the point of illegal aliens you're back to stereotyping -
back to the nannies and cleaning. You're back to a position
where men can do what they want because a lot of women will
tell you, that if you don't sleep with the guys, they'll go to the
American girls, and they'll dump you. A lot of women have felt
forced into a moral breaking away from traditional values and
that's hard on them.

It's just so male oriented. Everything is done through the
bars. The bars are only a place for women at certain times. For
example on a Friday evening it's not good for women to be seen
on the bar side of the bar, as opposed to the lounge side, which is
perfectly acceptable here! (Refers to bars in areas like
Dorchester, Boston.)

There are certain behavioural norms coming to play as
regards what is acceptable and what is not - the restrictions are
all on the women. I find none on the men. The drinking is huge
and it's a man's world over here (for Irish men), without a doubt.

A lot of friends were very good to me. One extremely good

friend, she pulled me through everything financial. And the church definitely. It came to me. They offered me everything. There was no question that anything that was needed was there.

America has a lot to offer about bringing up kids. The balance would go in favor of America if you think about it from the point of view of drink, depression. If I bring them up in Ireland, I'm rearing them for the boat. America, there's so much against you, but there's so much for you. It's what you take yourself.

When we got divorced we were both separate entities so therefore I didn't come under him any longer. So, I had to make my own case, and I did. At least if you have an attorney he can keep you in the country longer.

In America I think you're allowed to act a little differently. Not allowed, it's that you get to a stage and you grow up and decide that you are going to commit yourself to being this (divorced). I don't feel any pressure from society. I have felt a bit in very Irish circles, but I don't even notice it now.

Irish women here are not clubbing together. I've tried on one occasion to get a kind of a thing going with women. Everybody is for themselves. There's that fear, the tightening up when you come; the turning of husband to wife. It can improve a marriage initially to emigrate, because one turns to the other for support. But, there's that awful fear that if you start to look after other people you'll lose a grip on what it is you first set out to look after. People move because they can't pay mortgages. People move for money and that's the core of the whole thing.

They don't move because they want to move, particularly if they have children. Take the woman with a couple of kids - she comes over ...her husband and her children are her life. They're the people she's left for - she's had enough. Women are in their own units small and extended. I wouldn't say women are divided, they're not mixing enough together.

I won't go back to Ireland. I've never been back - I've severed all ties emotionally. I keep in contact but my family is dispersed. I have a commitment not just to America but to integrating into society. Everything in Ireland is centered around drink. It's just my recollection maybe - everything was drink and the "craic" and the drunker everybody is the funnier everybody is. But I don't see it like that, there's so much more to be done, there are so many things to do.

It's up to women themselves to get out and just do it. I like to think our daughters will. The community ("New Irish") now has been established and even if the law does change it will take time for the whole social thing to change for women. It's up to yourself - fight your own corner. I think women should stand up and just say "We're not taking this!"

BB

Ma, this is the way I am.

8 U.S.C. # 1182 (a)(4) excludes "[a]liens afflicted with psychopathic personality, or sexual deviation, or a mental defect." This provision has its origins in the Immigration Act of 1917, which excludes all aliens "of constitutional psychopathic personality."[28]

BB, a lesbian, grew up in Finglas, a suburb of Dublin. After school she qualified as a teacher of physical education and taught for a number of years Ireland and later in New York city. She emigrated to the United States in 1984 and lived for some years in New York. She now lives in Provincetown on Cape Cod and works in stained glass. She is deeply committed to the twelve-step programme for alcoholics. She is one of the bravest souls I have encountered in the course of this study and a model of the kind of courage it takes to be in charge and productive in the world.

When I was growing up there was only one parish which was just Finglas, by the time I left secondary school, there were four parishes. It went from a resident population of say fifteen thousand to about eighty thousand, in the space of ten years. There were many changes during that time- a huge influx of families and a lot of construction, building on a lot of parks where I used to play as a kid. Overall, my family had a great tradition in Finglas, my mother's side goes back - my great, great grandmother was a midwife in Finglas. My Dad was fourteen when he left school and started out as a messenger boy. He worked his way up in the same company he retired in as cost accountant.

Generally most of the girls in my class were ... their aim was to get married. Little thoughts of career, into teaching, nursing or being a housewife, that was the trend within the career counselling. I had a lot of sporting outlets at the time, mainly through school. The local camogie club got me out a lot. I really enjoyed growing up with that whole emphasis on sport. I was very much supported.

I choose PE (Physical Education) in second year in secondary school because of my interest in sports. This is what I focused my energy on in secondary school. I actually got my degree though I was repeating exams and that. I came out as a lesbian in my final year in College, to friends. I became aware that members of the faculty had also got wind of me being out as a lesbian and I think that contributed a lot to the kind of, what I consider abuse.

Then there was a fear, a general fear in myself against society because it was not accepted, it was not approved (lesbianism). There was fear around getting a permanent teaching position, because of signing a moral contract. I was going against everything in my own conscience in terms of the way I was brought up socially, religiously, politically. I felt I was breaking every rule in the book, but I just knew I had to do it for myself.

I'd always felt this way towards women as far back as I can remember. There was never the support system for it growing up. Even within school I remember within my third year within secondary school there was a religion book out called *The Moral Life* which was meant to be quite liberal in religious education. There was a section on relationships. I remember putting up my hand, I was really scared and I asked the teacher "How come there is no mention of homosexuality?" Her answer was "Because it doesn't exist, therefore it is not to be discussed." So, that was the end to my further questioning it.

I had no problem teaching in religious institutions because I believed what I was teaching was good quality and that my sexuality had no bearing on my work performance. That's the way I approached any interview I went for, I had no difficulty. Within any work situation I had no real difficulty except at times feeling isolated in faculty rooms when everyone else was talking about marriages, and couples.

Dublin was where I was introduced to the lesbian scene. I found it quite supportive. I first called a number in *In Dublin* magazine, and it was the Gay Information Network. It was very supportive in introducing me to another side of life I didn't really believe existed. I thought I was probably the only lesbian in Ireland, never mind Dublin. Unfortunately it was very much around the bar scene, three pubs - The Viking, which I think no longer exists, JJ Smyths, which is only Thursday nights and Saturday night and The Foggy Dew.

I came here (United States) in 1980 as a student. I worked in Atlantic City in the Irish community for four months. I was out to myself, but not out to friends and family. I had fun. I came back the following year, again for three months to Galveston, Texas. I think we were the only four Irish people on the whole island.

I came out (declared her sexuality) in 1982 after the last visit to the United States. It was never actually talked about, I never sat down and said "Ma, this is the way I am." My mother did ask me was I a lesbian when I was seventeen. I didn't feel ready to answer even then. I just kept silent. She insisted, so finally I said "No." She left it at that. However, along the way both my parents and family just realised it and it was just not talked about. My women lovers were always welcome at home. I was never questioned about being with men. So, I just decided it was better left alone.

Back in 1984 I returned to New York. I blended into the community. I moved out to San Francisco. My mother at this point was dying of cancer. I returned to Ireland. After she died I hung out in Ireland then moved back to New York (1986). It was there I decided I was tired of being an illegal alien and not having the opportunities, and the worry about going back to Ireland. I decided to teach. There was no problem getting work. The catholic archdiocese were very short of teachers. I enjoyed teaching. A year into the system I couldn't handle the numbers - the first year seven hundred (students) a week, nine periods a day of forty minutes. I could barely maintain a good living in New York city, but it meant more to me to have that freedom of choice.

My second year (was) when I had no central focus that was my own. I felt myself becoming a machine almost - getting up every day, going constant for a year. It got to a point where I knew that for my own sense of who I am, I had to stop. I made quite a few friends through teaching. People who would take me as I am and if they asked me about it (lesbianism) I'd just say

"I'm with women." I came to the Cape for vacation. I went back and decided I had to leave New York.

Two friends had worked in this place called Provincetown. I had heard that it had quite a large gay population, an artist's colony. I seemed a nice idea, a fishing village by the sea, perfect. I arrived in 1988 and bumped into a friend from College on the street one day. It was through spending a lot of time with herself and her boyfriend that I began to realise that there was something for me beyond what I was doing.

Looking back, my consumption of alcohol hadn't changed, but what changed was the amount it took for me to go over the edge. It used to be about six or eight pints, and I was still functioning, whereas it was beginning to take about three pints and I would sometimes go into a complete personality change. I had often heard of alcoholism, but denied myself it in my brain.

It's often with minority groups, oppressed groups that you'll find addictions - drug addictions, alcoholism. As a lesbian and a gay community our society makes us feel isolated. Therefore we isolate together and to deal with that isolation often I think men and women turn to either drugs or alcohol. Because that kind of loneliness over the years can just build up to a point where alcohol changes one's perception of reality. I was an active alcoholic. In recovery I see a completely different side, the endless amount of support for people.

I always had this thing for the Arts. I loved making things with my hands. Once the drinking took over in my early twenties most of the creative outlet was gone. It stopped developing at that point. I think part of giving up alcohol I had to focus my energy. I began to take stained glass classes. I found a great affinity for glass, really enjoyed it. I perceive it like painting, making scenes with glass. A local stained glass shop asked if I'd be interested in being an apprentice. I have a small workshop in my own home and sell my work in Boston, in Harvard Square and in Provincetown. I've developed my own very recognisable style. My company is called *Gloine Gleoite*, which means Beautiful Glass.

Here there's the fear that there may be exposure (of her sexuality). As far as I know, they will not allow an open homosexual into this country. It's another form of being excluded, discriminated against. I mean, I am who I am. The way I feel today is that I don't have a choice in being straight. I just have to accept who I am for me. To hell with it! Who I am is very important to me - I love women. It's not all of my life, but a very important part and if I can't have that openly and feel comfortable with it, I'll go back home if they deport me.

Fionnuala McKenna

Fionnuala McKenna is a young Irish woman who in 1988 established the New Irish Theatre Company in Boston. Her troupe consists of Irish immigrants, mostly like herself, "illegals", undocumented. None of them had experience of theatre in Ireland. To date they have produced O'Casey's *Juno and the Paycock*, and Brian Friel's *Philadelphia Here I Come!* Their next production will be *The Hiker* by John B Keane. Fionnuala also works for her own painting company and on plans for an Irish Arts Centre for Boston.

I was born in Manorhamilton, County Leitrim the seventh child of seven children in 1964. After national school I went to Ballyshannon County Donegal to secondary (school). I was there as a boarder, it was nineteen miles away. So, I used to come home at weekends. It was kind of a tradition that we all went to boarding school. It was less expensive to send us to boarding school then than to actually keep us at home - about eighty pounds a term. The secondary school was run by the Mercy nuns.

At seventeen I didn't particularly want to go to College because I didn't particularly enjoy school. So, I went to France for a couple of weeks during the summer. I was interested in working with kids. I got a job in Sligo Day Care Centre which facilitated deprived kids. I worked there under a Youth Employment Scheme, or Manpower Scheme as it was then, for the huge sum of twenty pounds a week. I lived with my sister. Then I took off for the summer, went to Greece for a couple of weeks. I had applied for a few colleges during the year. I was eighteen and accepted into Galway for Civil Engineering, Dublin for Environmental Studies and Sligo for Child Care. I particularly didn't want to stay at home.

I chose Dublin because I got a grant to go there. I barely survived on my grant. In April I realised that it was a pathetic course and out of a class of twenty three, I think four stayed in it. It was very badly run. I dropped out and signed on the dole.

Thought it was wonderful for a couple of weeks until I got totally bored. Then I started getting worried about what I was going to do. At that stage I was nineteen and I went through a very severe state of depression. I was under a lot of family pressure about what I was going to do. Here I was wandering around with nothing and everybody seemed to be doing something. I didn't have any answers and I didn't know what I wanted to do, but I knew I wanted to get away from something.

My eldest sister was very helpful. She asked me what I really wanted to do, which was Montessori teaching. I hadn't the confidence to think that I was able to do that because I just didn't feel I was capable of it, intellectually. I never worked that much in school because I wasn't interested that much in what I was taught. I don't think my mother had that much confidence in me. There was always that drive to do well and I think I just rebelled against it. I knew deep down I didn't have any funding. I wasn't going to get any unless I did what my mother wanted me to do. So, I was left in a dilemma. My sister said she would fund me to do Montessori. She had the trust that I would do it. I applied to London and I was accepted. She gave me a loan and it was the best thing that ever happened. As soon as I went to London all the depression that I had gone through that summer and frustration and everything else just vanished. I was in a new environment and I was starting from scratch - I flourished.

I got my qualification and then I got a job out in Greece. I didn't really know what it was till I got out there. It ended up more or less as a babysitter whereas I understood I was to be a teacher to the kids. After three weeks I decided this was crazy. I was determined to stay there for a year, so I got a job teaching English. In Greece I saw so much wealth in certain families. I decided I would prefer that my skills were used for other kids who can't afford it - deprived or emotionally disturbed. I decided to go home to Ireland. It was very frustrating. I spent six months - three months of doing absolutely nothing except ringing up places and tearing up the yellow pages. That was in 1985. So, in September I got on another scheme as an assistant in a national school with kids who were mildly mentally handicapped. Then I got a job with the ISPCC (Irish Society for the Prevention of Cruelty to Children). That I really enjoyed very much.

I went over to America for holidays. My brother was going through a hard emotional time - a divorce, in El Paso, Texas. I passed through Boston on the way home and it inspired me to come over more than anything. It was the height of the summer and everything looked rosy. I was just taken back by all the WANT signs in 1986. I started work again with the ISPCC until December. I had to make a choice there and then because I was earning sixty eight pounds a week. I was reduced to cycling everywhere and had to move out of the house and move in with my sister and her husband. I was getting fed up with this. In Greece I was earning a salary that was a lot better than what I had in Ireland. Once that happens you, you don't want to regress, you'd like to go on a bit. So, I decided that perhaps I would go to college in London. My plan was to go to America for six months and apply to London and start a social work course.

I handed in my resignation at the ISPCC. Also, I explained why I was leaving and that I thought it was a shame we were losing people who were dedicated to teaching because of pay.

I arrived in America in January of 1987. It was very different to the Boston I saw in the summer of 1986. I mean, God Almighty, I was knee deep in snow. There weren't any signs that I saw before (for work). I came to South Boston. It wasn't a great apartment either. I just bunked on the floor. I think I had four hundred dollars and I automatically assumed that within a week I was going to get a job. Little did I know that three months later I still wouldn't have a job. I thought I was depressed before, but I never was as near to having a nervous breakdown as I was that time. For the first time in my life I really was disappointed with myself and my own judgement.

I used to get a day here and a day there temping - photocopying or something. I used to walk everywhere. My friend didn't know anybody because her schedule was geared towards the evening shift, four to twelve. So, her social life was extremely limited. I do remember going to the Kinvara (Irish pub) once and I just thought it was so far away, so out of bounds. I saw these people sitting at the bar. I couldn't approach them. I couldn't say "Hi, I'm from Ireland" because it was obvious that they were from Ireland and then what do you do? I was like a little kid waiting for somebody to take me by the hand and say "Listen, this is my phone number, give me a call." But it never happened.

I did meet two people in South Boston from the Aran Islands. They invited me to a party. I was introduced to the woman next door who was babysitting. We just seemed to click and we met the next day to go out for a run. One thing led to another. She was involved with the camogie team. In the matter of a week it was as if the clouds opened and I saw a bright blue sky.

I had been working one month in an insurance company at that stage, illegally. They had asked me for my papers as they had to do, of course I had nothing to furnish them with, so, I had to disappear. I got a painting job the following week through an ad in the paper. An American guy said that his mother said he was to employ me because I was a woman. She heard the Irish voice on the answering machine and I think she was of Irish extraction. I was immediately in a different type of workforce. It was very male orientated. I was the only woman in the whole building. I spent a couple of months with him. Through that I started getting very confident asking people for work painting. Once I was in painting it was very easy to get work. It was a good experience for me to know just how men work. Then in September I started working on my own and I did a couple of jobs there.

I liked the independence of me choosing my own hours and I could work better. That Christmas I went down to visit my brother. When I came back I realised that I was unemployed. I went through six weeks in January of 1988 not having any work. So, a pattern started to formulate.

In October of 1987 I got totally disillusioned with what was happening here in Boston. When I was at home I was involved in a lot of groups - women's groups and political groups. I was just very active on a social level about what was going on with the government. There was just a void here. It was all going to the pub and having the pints and it was great - you were earning. The whole social thing was very different and I was missing something. I thought "Wouldn't it be great to put on a play?" It's a good forum to show to people in a way that's not too dogmatic. You're not forcing people to watch so therefore they come out of their own will and take from it what they want. It's open to many interpretations. Getting people in a group was a way of throwing out ideas too. In the matter of a few weeks I got about fifteen names together. I got someone who was interested in directing. Nobody had any experience at all. They were all Irish immigrants, mostly illegal. So, through trial and error we managed to pull ourselves together. By the following April we had the *Juno and the Paycock* in production. It was great - everybody who came to see it was blown away by it. That stirred something in people, they wanted to go on and develop.

Then I choose *Philadelphia Here I Come!* It was a play that people were familiar with. *Juno and the Paycock* with the reputation that O'Casey has, I figured it was a good play to do. I thought it was a good way to build up a reputation until such a stage that you could branch out and do your own work. I spend about twenty to twenty five hours a week actually planning things and keeping myself three or four steps ahead of where we are. In that sense I'm responsible for the development of The New Irish Theatre.

I see Boston as home to thirty thousand Irish immigrants (refers to New Irish). To me it seems crazy that there is no facility in the area for the Arts. In New York, San Francisco and St Paul you have an Arts Centre. I think people have the ideas to do it, but not the determination to carry it through. I will do it. I want a premises whereby artists, not just people in theatre, can be at home - potters, painters, sculptors. A venue whereby we could bring over artists from Ireland to keep people in touch with what is happening there. Also, if there is money here, some of it can be pumped into art in Ireland. It's probably through that close connection with my sisters, professional artists in Ireland, that I have a deep love for it as well. I know the struggles and the hardship that people go through for the little recognition that they get.

If I was given a lump sum this is what I would do. I would have a centre that would have in it an auditorium for the theatre to take place and also for poetry reading; a hallway for exhibitions; a couple of rooms where Irish or any classes could take place. I would most definitely have a creche in it and workshops with kids at weekends - puppets, masks whatever. I'd like space in the basement for musicians so they don't have to rely on people's apartments. I would like next year (1991) to have a building with at least a theatre in it.

I must say America has released a valve in me, just like the steam of a kettle, its (creativity) constantly pouring out. Whether it's just the isolation of being totally on my own, independent, away from family has done it or whether it's the struggle involved with being here and having to fight for survival, has caused me to be more determined.....I suppose there are many factors really. I don't sense the depression here that I do at home. I felt strangled at home. I was just held back.

Boston is becoming a home to many people and you can see from the number of kids that are being born to couples who have arrived within the last five or six years. A real feeling of settlement is coming over people. That inspired me even more in my drive to form something. I'll be here for the next ten years at least.

Rena Cody

Rena Cody, Immigrant and Refugee Outreach worker at Neponset Health Centre, Boston has carved a place for herself as *the* social worker to the Irish immigrant community in Boston. Rena left school at age fifteen to become a hairdresser. She returned years later to University College Cork to do her social work degree. Throughout her life she has been involved in community groups in rural and urban Ireland. She is a former member of the Irish Feminist Information Collective[29] and a founding member of an Irish Women in Boston Group. She runs weekly groups for Irish Women and Irish Women with children at Neponset.

B orn the first of November 1952, I am now thirty seven. In the family there were eleven children, six sisters and four brothers. I was born in Templemore, in County Tipperary and then when I was two my family moved to County Waterford. Then when I was around twelve or so I moved to Dublin.

My father had been in the army. My mother was apprenticed to an aunt of hers. My grand aunt owned a small grocery shop/restaurant in Templemore and when my father left the army he came into the shop. They left when I was two. The army left the town and the police hadn't moved in yet. There was very little business in the town and they couldn't support the shop.

In Waterford my father worked the paper mills, as a lab assistant. My mother was at home full-time with us. I remember my father having to work really, really hard. He worked shift work and the negative side of it was I can remember just how tired he used to be and the hours he used to work. My aunt Katie came to live with us, she who had owned the shop. She helped rear us. It was quite a drop in social status for my mother. She had lost a lot, both her own identity as a businesswoman which she loved, and a lot of prestige. I've heard stories and she was regretful, and angry at being poor. She had never been that well off, but she did have standing and a prestige, and much more middle class aspirations than my father.

I stayed there until I was eleven or twelve and then we moved to Dublin. It was my mother's decision. I think she saw that all her own family had emigrated to England, and she was very clear she didn't want the family to break up. Her whole identity then was to be a good mother, and she decided we were going to live in Dublin. With a couple of trips on the train she went in and negotiated a bank loan. I can remember the name of the bank manager, Tommy Doyle, in Dublin. It was she who also planned to buy a house and get back into business, which she did. Then my father took a job in another paper factory in Dublin. But my mother bought a three bedroom house that had a garage beside it with a plan of setting my sister, the hairdresser, up in business.

I did my Inter Cert (examination) at thirteen. I think I would have been fourteen that November and I left in June. I wanted to get out of school. I didn't like it very much. In the begining they used to make a lot of fun of me because I was from the country. There was also a certain amount of pressure from home, my family. My four elder brothers and sister were working at this stage. We had actually opened the hair dressing salon and extended the house. My mother used to do the books and my sister ran the business. So, I left partly as well because she had gotten engaged to be married. My family was keen to have somebody else come into the business. I apprenticed for about a year and a half in Grafton Street and finished with my sister. When she got married, I took over the business. I was seventeen or so.

I left it when I was twenty three. I was a volunteer youth worker for years. I lived in Artane and was a volunteer in one of the first working class housing estates to be built in the Coolock suburbs. I became more and more interested in youth work. I loved it and wanted to get out of the salon and away from my family - away from home and responsibility.

I applied for the Irish Poverty Program and to my amazement, I got the job. Within the space of about two weeks I had gone from being a hairdresser to being a community organiser. I worked for four years in a rural poverty programme in Castletownbere in West Cork. I worked with small rural fishermen, farmers - small farmers, mixed youth clubs, men and

Fionnuala McKenna

Rena Cody
Photographs: Sandra McDade

women. Of the four years we were there (with a colleague, Patricia Kelleher) there were a lot of mixed feelings about people being called rural poverty workers. The idea of poverty in Ireland was something to be very ashamed of and the idea of looking at poverty in structural terms- people who were disadvantaged and didn't have access to power, education, the means of making their livlihood better for themselves - was quite a new concept, quite a radical idea in Ireland at the time. It was difficult for someone like myself who was quite new to the idea. Then translate it into working with other people.

The Programme actually closed down when the EEC funding ran out in 1980 and we were made redundant. I had bought a share in a house in Connemara and I lived there for nine months. The man I was living with was studying in Galway. A friend told me about a programme that was on in University College Cork which was a two year CQSW, a four year social work qualification in two years. You were allowed matriculate on the basis of experience. It was perfect for me.

Then I went back to Dublin in 1983. I wasn't entirely happy about moving back to the city. I worked as a social worker in the Adelaide Hospital and I stayed four years as a medical and psychiatric social worker. I left that job to come to the USA.

In terms of family, there was no history of my people coming to America. The one person I knew was a man Mike Miller, who had been an advisor to the Irish Poverty Programme. I'd also met his wife, Jean Baker Miller, when she came to Dublin. I really felt I needed to get some private space in my life. I think I came to realise some sense of myself, some creative side of myself that I wansn't able to get in touch with in Ireland. This was really a history for me coming from a really large family. My mother was widowed and I felt a fair responsibility, warranted or not, to take care of her in some ways. I came in November 1987.

I sold the share I had in a house, that's how I financed the trip. I think at gut level I knew I was coming for quite some time, several years. The first couple of months I was very tired and quite burnt out in many ways from my work. I traveled on the Greyhounds for about three months. I came back to Boston and I'd heard about the difficulties of the undocumented Irish. I said I'd see if there was anybody doing that kind of work and I needed to get a job. I did go to the Irish Embassy and was very discouraged. I started calling around the Health Centres. The neighbourhood I picked was Dorchester. I also had heard of the Irish Immigration Reform Movement. I went out, met them and said "Do you reach people on a social problems?" They said "We're a political lobbying organistaion." So, they had a telephone line where people would call in and I offered to work on the line. Myself and Odette Harrington developed the Help Line. I volunteered with them for a couple of months and we used to call around in Dorchester. Eventually one of the neighbourhood health centres, Neponset Health Centre, called me and said would I like to come for interview. They offered me a consultancy job for six months to do outreach work, to look at the immigrant and refugee population within the area. I was very excited about it as this meant not just working with Irish immigrants but with all the populations in Boston as well.

Then I went looking for a lawyer to be told I couldn't get sponsored for six months. It appeared that my qualification from Ireland didn't actually make me eligible for the H1 visa. Eventually I found a young woman lawyer and she said she'd take a risk with me. It took us three months. In the meantime I'd volunteered while all this process was going on, trying to keep the job open. I got the visa three or four days before Christmas.

What's one of the interesting things to find is that a lot of what I thought was there, is there. A lot of isolation, loneliness, things indeed that I experienced myself. A fair amount of alcohol abuse, especially among young people. A high amount of pregnancies amongst single women. Couples living together who are undocumented and decide to have children. Can't get access to health care, who are afraid to come in for services. Some psychological issues on mental health. I've had two people who have actually had serious mental breakdowns.

People come for all sorts of reasons. It's facinating to look at. No more than myself, they have mixed and often unclear notions of why they come over. People come because they think it will cure a relationshiop that's been rocky. People come because they want to make more money and a better life. People wanting to get out of Ireland to be indpendent. To have an income of your own is the most obvious one, but the underbelly of that, all the time, is to have space and independence away from your culture, away from the 'valley of the squinting windows' kind of thing.

For women, probably one of the biggest things is that they have an independent income of their own and an apartment to share with other women, which they certainly couldn't have

afforded on the dole or low-paying jobs in Ireland. For a lot it
means sexual freedom. You can actually be with men or women,
to explore in an adult way options in your life. For some people
you have less responsibilities around your families. What's
interesting, looking at some of the women, is that the older
women, some of the 'Donnelly' visas have been caretakers in
their family.

For some people it was just a very crude stark reality,
particularly for west of Ireland and some of the midland rural
people, that there was no work, and that there was no work in
sight (in Ireland).

You don't know what it's like to be undocumented unless
somebody had told you and it's only now, four or five years
down the road that it's being spoken about. Even still, people
find it very hard to go home and talk about it because the myth is
that you've come to America to be a success. You're not going to
go home and say it isn't working out, or it's painfully hard or "I
mind some upper class family's children in Newton or Wellsley
and it's as lonely as hell all day." Three or four years down the
road it's not a holiday anymore, not fun, and that's what I'm
seeing more of now.

I set up with a colleague, an Irish Immigrant Women's
Discussion Group on Monday nights at the Health Centre and
we've had twenty six women there of a night. None of us realised
how lonely and isolated it is. I think there's some very exciting,
fabulous stuff happening for men and women here. Some very
liberating things. I think women are exploring sides of
themselves including myself, that you don't often do at home.
People are studying and in therapy.

I think it's impossible to do psychotherapy as a therapist
unless you have experienced it yourself. I couldn't possibly sit
and listen to immigrant stories, mostly women which is
inevitable - women come into therapy first and then haul their
male partners in after them. Women are usually more open to
that. We've not been allowed to express our feelings as a culture.
We come from a very rigid culture in many ways. I think our
sexuality is very repressed and they are some of the reasons
people leave is to get out and be freer of those kinds of attitudes.
Some people can do it at home, I'm not saying one has to leave
to to achieve or liberate some of that in yourself. Personally, I
couldn't. I needed to leave. If I'm ready to go home, then I go
home.

I think there is a very high price being paid in Ireland, both emotionally and creatively. 42,000 people left Ireland last year (1988) under the age of about thirty six. That's an extraordinary loss of the kind of radical energy of young people who need to change a society that is very restrictive. One of my reasons as well for coming away was to look at that. We'd lost a divorce referendum, we'd lost an abortion referendum, we were going further back in terms of just choices especially those open to women. We've only had access to contraception in my lifetime. As a single woman in Ireland the options socially and culturally open to me, even to meet new people, new partners in your thirties is very difficult. And not that it's actually hugely more easy in the States, but at least there are wider choices.

A lot of people want to go home. A lot of people genuinely want to, are saying 'its ok to be here, I make lots of money', but they'll say things like 'I don't want to marry in America' and if they do 'The last thing I want to do is have children in this society.' However, with the new legislation it's getting very frightening for a State (Massachusetts) that is known for its hospitable approach to immigrants and refugees. State funding will stop because of the fiscal crisis. With that atmosphere there will be a backlash in terms of undocumented people.

For now I'm very happy to be doing what I'm doing. I like it a lot. I have basically created a job which has the two sides of my experience - community organizing and direct social services, therapy work. But in time I would actually like to study again. In my head I'm saying I'm here for a couple of years and the Health Centre has offered to sponsor me for three or four years. I'm still an emigrant. I still have all the emotions and feelings that all the people who come to see me have. I couldn't honestly say now that I could see myself not returning to Ireland.

Máire Ní Bhranlaigh

If you could make a few bob at it at all,
it would be a great life.

Born in Sligo town twenty eight years ago, Máire Ní Bhranlaigh was the eldest girl in a family of five children. After a difficult presonal educational experience, Máire vowed that her teaching

would be for those "who have been failing all along." She
emigrated in 1986 at the height of the eighties flight. Here she
has blossomed as a writer, becoming in my opinion the voice of
the new immigrant Irish woman. Máire lives in Brighton with
Claudia, two goldfish - "Star" and "Stripe" - "Ginger" the cat,
"Pepper" the dog. She has no plans to return long-term to
Ireland. Her book *Taking the boat* will be published in 1990.

My mother came from Sligo. She was a junior assistant
mistress (teacher) at the foot of Benbulben, Log na Gall.
My first rub with religious education was with the Mercys. In
school we just got the dog's abuse from morning till night. The
principal of the school (secondary) was a very narrowminded,
bitter, frustrated woman. I'm sure there's quite a long name for
what's her problem. The constant abuse was over uniforms. It
was idiotic. We had to wear slippers 'cause it was a new school
and it had to be kept in pristine condition for the next hundred
years. A ridiculous thing. The school itself looked like a space
module. The central dome was supposedly a library, but we
didn't know if it was a library or not because we never got to put
a foot in it. 'Twas a library alright, but the doors were always
locked. "We don't want any of the girls in messing up the
books."

I was mad to go to Galway to do a degree in Psychology, but
my mother said that she thought it a much better idea if I went to
St Pat's (teacher training college in Dublin), where there was a
major subsidy going for national school teachers. There was that
or nursing. There weren't any other options presented as being
within the realm of possibility. I didn't have any choice. That's
the way I felt about it. I remember some of the Dubs laughing at
me because I was a right culchie - I'd never fail to look up when
the airplanes passed. I found the transition very hard. I couldn't
stand another nun, that's the basic reason I went to St Pat's. All
the Mercy girls went to Carysfort.

My first job was in Manorhamilton in 1982. I was full of
good ideas, all sorts of projects; singsongs night, noon and
morning. I really enjoyed them. Then, I got the enviable
permanent and pensionable job teaching sixth class. I wanted
them to understand that I respected them and that whatever level
they were at was fine. I didn't have this standard of "everybody
has to be able to do this", because everybody is not able to
achieve to the required level. So that my bias was always, and is

always, the students who have been failing all along. That's the love of my life right there.

In 1985, in that summer I had come out to the States with some friends and we'd spent the summer painting. When I went back in September I couldn't settle. I was saying "I have to get out of this place." That was also the year of the strike proceedings for all the teachers. There were a lot of rallies. We weren't getting our proper raise. It will tell you how fed up everybody was because there was almost a 99% adherence to the strike days. For the month of March we were on strike three days of every week. It was a very strong statement.

This was a 'push' factor, coupled with the auld referendum on the rights of the unborn. I mean, that was a particularly sickening affair. That was absolutely galling for me at the time because I had had an abortion in March and I was very fragile. I saw the weight of public opinion very much against what I had done. Particularly being a national school teacher, being in a very conservative occupation. The tide in Ireland was becoming more and more conservative. As we slipped into deeper recession and depression I think everybody was sort of guilt-ridden and saying "we have to get back to the days of former innocence." Yes, it was absolutly anti-woman. The whole catholic church is incredibly anti-woman. It's control of women's bodies.

I had taken a year off and the plan was to come to America, make money and head for Australia. I just knew it had to be better from where I was leaving. But also I left knowing that I wouldn't be returning. In the back of my mind it was different, 'cause I knew I wasn't just going off for a year. This was a hidden agenda, but it was unspoken. Anything I had I sold.

We knew if we came to Boston we'd be ok for accomodation 'cause my uncle said he'd be able to give us an apartment in Cambridge. We thought, "sure we'll find some auld job anyway, to get the start." My uncle had a friend who wanted his "mansions" in Chelsea renovated. We got the job painting for five dollars an hour, in the Puerto-Rican Gaeltacht. I was facinated by all the different kinds of people. We three had a very sheltered life in terms of the homogeneous society in Ireland.

I had been in a fury all summer. After the abortion I hadn't gotten over it. I didn't feel any support from my friends. I was furious to realise I really didn't have the friends I thought I had.

At the end of the summer we set off for New York. I was more or less reluctantly sticking to the idea of Australia, but with typical Irish articulation, was mute about the whole thing. (To find work) Margaret was well able for the "craic." She'd make up a pack of lies. I'd get on the phone, I'd be stuttering and muttering. People thought I was an absolute idiot. I just couldn't rev up into fourth gear to put on the necessary act. I was illegal and just could not bring myself to do what was expected.

I did get a job minding this child in Manhatten. I was hired as a sort of governess, mar dhea (my eye). I spent far more time cleaning and scrubbing. They lived in luxury. I lived in a very small space. 'Twas great money, bed and board. I really resented this woman. She treated me as such an inferior being that the whole set up got on my nerves. I couldn't stand it. I went back to Boston. I didn't want to stay in the States and be arsing around nannying.

My uncle called me up before New Year's Day to say "We need a manager (for a Motel). Do you want the job?" It was in York Beach, Maine. All of a sudden I had a purpose and the wherewithal or reason to stay. I was at the motel for twenty months - a thirty six room motel. There was a lot of responsibility - from bookwork, to balancing the chequebook, to marketing, everything. It was very, very miserable. I was a basket case. I had no one to talk to. I was really suffering from depression and was unable to think clearly, to get myself out of the situation.

Through the encouragement of a friend I got my act together in April. She said "Go and get yourself a teaching job, get legal and here's how to do it." I flew home to collect my visa (H1) and then back to teach. This is my second year at Cathedral Grammar, an inner city school. It's multi-cultural - you name it, they're in our school - Hispanics, Asians, Nigerians, Greeks and a few Italians. I'm the token "Paddy." It's wonderful. I'm really 100% there trying to enable them, give them some feeling of success and a true sense of what they're worth.

I have grown up here - not only as a writer. I found an outlet for all my frustration and loneliness in writing. I came to Boston and got myself into a journal writing group at the Women's Centre. Through all the exercises I developed a voice, or began to understand my own ability to re-member and to write. I got a taste of what writing full-time was like this summer, because I took the summer off. It was just so different and so great. If you could make a few bob at it at all, it would be a great life.

Chapter Seven
Generations of Daughters

As can be seen from the words of the 1980s women, the issues can often be similar and the struggles as difficult as those of earlier generations of daughters. Therefore, it is important for the oral information to flow as constantly as the waves of female migration. The words must become the matrix and source of strength in this matrilineal process as women in the 1980s and 1990s learn from the models in whose steps they follow.

The vast majority of these 1980s women are unaware of their part in the story of Irish women's migration to the USA. The story is alluded to in the Irish-language novel on the Leaving Certificate syllabus of every Irish student: *Peig*, the transcribed reminiscences of an old Kerry woman, Peig Sayers. Peig's best friend, Cáit Jim, emigrates to America with the intention of earning enough money to send the price of the fare home to Peig but their plan fails when Cáit Jim breaks her hand and cannot work. Peig goes back "in aimsir," as a servant, until an arranged marriage.

This scant reference is the only clue given to modern Irish women to the unique story-chain that lies behind the tale of Peig and Cáit Jim. Because Irish women of the 1990s do not know their history they will be bereft of role models until these women's lives are recorded, a process which has only just begun within the past decade.[30] Until they have such models and stories, they will continue to be unable to make the links between the reasons why these women left Ireland and the reasons for the present exodus of Irish women. In America, Irish women feel alienated from a culture and a history that the Irish American community indulges. While the role of the Irish male in politics is praised and eulogised and monuments are erected in their honour in cities across the USA, scant reference if any is made to the proud legacy of labour activists Elizabeth Gurley Flynn or Cork woman Mother Jones or indeed to the thousands of Irish women who worked, sweated and lived together in the dusty mills of Lowell.

The veneration of Irish male immigrants and the acclamation their success stories receive belie the fact that significantly more Irish women than men have come through the "golden door." Even the day most associated with the Irish in America is celebrated in the honour of St Patrick, who was neither an Irishman nor Ireland's first native saint. That was St Brighid, whose name became the stereotype of Irish women in America - Irish women emigrants were called 'Brigids' and especially when in domestic service. Perhaps this will change when the Irish women of the 1990s come to know and understand the rich legacy of which they are a part.

Lives of their Choosing

The histories presented here provide role models of women who led lives of their choosing, rather than that which was prescribed for them. As daughters, cousins, and aunts their lives provide us with the models of "Brighids" for future generations who may chose to remain in Ireland or depart.

However, in reclaiming the proud role models we must not forget the casualties of the process of emigration, those who do not appear here. I recall especially Helen from Co Mayo who on the day I visited was in a one room home in a boarding house. Surrounding her in "Store 24" plastic bags were her entire life's possessions. She had spent her whole life bringing relatives to the USA and sent money home to keep the family going. Now, in the twilight of her days she sat lost in a lonely emigrants' limbo - neither here nor there - alone, and quite mad.

In listening to the histories of these emigrant women we begin a process of recognition and reclamation. What is hopeful is that some models are beginning to be remembered publically - Anne Glover, Irish woman and witch who was hanged in the South End of Boston on 16 November, 1688, just over three hundred years ago. She has been awarded the distinction of "Goody Glover Day" in Boston by the Boston City Council (16 November, 1988).

In conclusion then, these stories show that long before the words of a woman (Emma Lazarus), on the statue of a woman (Liberty) drew hundreds of thousands of the "huddled masses yearning to breath free," Irish women have chosen to come to America. Indeed it should be remembered that an Irish woman, Annie Moore, was in fact the first person through Ellis Island. This movement must be viewed as one of empowerment rather than defeat. In choosing to come to the USA Irish women have long shown a desire to seek more than was allocated them at home. The paths these women have chosen are different, as different as the women themselves and in that regard we must listen to their words and avoid over-generalisation.

However, some elements in the story are undeniable. The message we can take from these women is "*misneach*/courage." They did not make the relatively short trip to seek a new life in Britain, but they made a decision that meant a more long-term if not, for some earlier emigrants, a final separation from their homeland.

By their rejection of Irish society, a society oppressive to women, Irish women turned their backs on Ireland and chose to move to the USA. As I listened to women's voices I have learned that though this may be so, emigrants from all three waves are strongly bonded with Ireland, and ideally, given the right conditions and the right opportunity for women, they would return. I also suggested that the rejection of family life was a major theme in the story of Irish women emigrants to the USA. It was and is, but not necessarily one to be elevated above those who chose family life. Those who did, did so on their own terms.

In my analysis of Ireland in the 1950s I stressed the negative role of the catholic church and its impact or push to emigrant women in that decade. This I believe to be correct; however, these emigrant women have nonetheless retained a very strong spiritual dimension to their lives, a dimension that may require the ritual and place of worship that the catholic church in America offers. In this sense they have retained their links with the patriarchal church, but again very much on their own terms.

This century has seen three generations of daughters leave Ireland. The reasons made for this self-imposed exile cannot fall under the simple blanket statement that there were no jobs. As the life stories of Irish women emigrants make abundantly clear, America provides Irish women the opportunity to achieve "a wider vision of ourselves," as 1980s emigrant Rena Cody puts it.

For Irish women in America today, especially at a time when technology is advancing at such a rate that people are leaving fewer and fewer written records, the need for oral histories is beyond doubt. To listen is to learn and to learn is to understand. By listening to the models presented here, the merest taste of all the stories to be told and heard, by understanding their words, major movement / growth can occur in individual women's lives and ultimately in the lives of all Irish women.

The Brighids of generations of Irish women have transported to America the Goddess of healing, smiths, fertility and poetry as their symbol. Indeed, no better model could be available to us, for the elements in Brighid's power have been evidenced in the stories of the lives of Irish women heard here, and those we have yet to hear - the healing, their strength, the fire of the smith to blaze a trail in the face of adversity, their fertility in the generations of women who follow one another, and the poetry, their voices.

The author, Ide O'Carroll,
with 1920s emigrant, Mary Terry Kelly.
Photograph: Caitríona Cooke

Notes

1   Gordon, Linda 'What's New in Women's History?' *Feminist Studies - Critical Studies* de Lauretis, Teresa (ed) Indiana, 1986 p. 24.
2   The English-born Countess Markievicz, active in the Easter Rising, became first woman member of British Parliament. Under the de Valera Dáil she was appointed Minister for Labour. *See* Ward, Margaret *Unmanageable Revolutionaries: Women and Irish Nationalism*, 1983. Hanna Sheehy-Skeffington would publicly state her case in September 1920 - her nationalism came first. This philosophy is mirrored in the adherence of many northern women today whose loyalty is first and foremost to a nationalist creed, at the expense of nationalism. *See* Derry Film and Video, *Mother Ireland* (video).
3   *Hanna Sheehy-Skeffington: Irish Feminist* Levenson, Leah and Natterstad, Jerry H, 1986 p. 145.
4   "Of 899,000 females of twenty years and over recorded in the 1926 census, no less than 233,000, or over one-quarter, were widowed or single and without gainful employment." (Brown, Terence. *Ireland: A Social and Cultural History 1922-1979* Glasgow, 1981 p. 91).
5   Scheper-Hughes, Nancy *Saints, Scholars and Schizophrenics: Mental Illness in Rural Ireland* Berkeley 1979.
6   My correspondence from Patrick Long, Director, Kilmainham Gaol Museum (28 March, 1989) includes a copy of a document recording Bridie Halpin in Prison records. It reads "NDU June 1923. Bridie Halpin, Prisoner of War No. 294, Late of Kilmainham jail. NDU June 1923."

7   Ward, Margaret. *Unmanageable Revolutionaries: Women and Irish Nationalism*, 1983. See also Buckley, Margaret, *The Jangle of the Keys*. Dublin, 1938 (now out of print). I am indebted to Mike McCormick, National Historian for the Ancient Order of Hibernians for his invaluable help in putting me in contact with the Halpin family and for acquiring copies of the *Halpin Papers*, and a copy of *The Jangle of the Keys* for me. A short story by Mike on Bridie's life first appeared in the *Irish Echo* on April 2, 1988. Also, thanks to Christy and Noel Halpin, Bridie's nephews.

8   Cumann na mBan, Constitution, Corughadh. Published Kilmainham, Dublin, pamphlet, no date. *Halpin Papers*. See also Ward, *Unmanageable Revolutionaries*, pp.88-199.

9   Letter from Maud Gonne MacBride, Roebuck House, Clonskea, Co Dublin. 25 November, 1948 - Halpin Papers. For background on Maud Gonne MacBride see Ward, pp. 42-54. WB Yeats directed much of his love poetry to Maude Gonne with whom he was in love. She later married MacBride, father of Séan who would lead Clann na Phoblachta, the party of Dr Noel Browne (see chapter 5).

10   *Halpin Papers*. For an excellent account of how the women in the North Dublin Union and Kilmainham ran the prisons see *The Jangle of the Keys*.

11   Lecturing at Harvard (12 November 1988) Dr Mary Fitzgerald spoke of how Irish women nationalists at the start of the century were "naive readers" in that they took the aims of Irish nationalism literally and believed verbatim the 1916 Proclamation. Like Bridie they did not read it as an agenda which was open to any interpretation that might be made under compromising political circumstances. It appears that Bridie believed at this stage that the "cause" would remain unsettled until pressure from abroad could be brought to bear. I am indebted to Katherine O'Donnell for notes on the Fitzgerald lecture.

12   Passport of Bridie Halpin. *Halpin Papers*.

13   Letter from the American consulate, "Visa Refused under Authorization of Immigration Act of 1924. TS Barry. American Consul. 23 April, 1931." *Halpin Papers*.

14   Letter dated 25 November 1937 from Catholic Emigration Society, 65 Trafalgar Square, London to Bridie Halpin 57, Gladstone Street, SE1. *Halpin Papers*.

15 The papers of the Clann na Phoblachta branch that Bridie Halpin formed show only a handful of members and evidence that very little money was collected. *Halpin Papers*.
16 Interview with Christy Halpin, Bridie's nephew. Tape in *O'Carroll Collection*.
17 Comment by Noel Halpin, Bridie's nephew. Interview with the Halpin family, March 1989.
18 The *O'Carroll Collection* is my collection which will be housed in the Fall at the Murray Research Centre on Women, Radcliffe College, Cambridge, Mass.
19 Lee, JJ *Ireland 1945-1970* 1979 p. 120.
20 Browne, Terence *Ireland: A Social and Cultural History 1922-1979* p. 184
21 Crofts, William 'The Atlee Government's Pursuit of Women' in *History Today*, August 1986, pp. 29-35.
22 Ibid. p. 32
23 Litton, Frank (ed) 'The Changing Social Structure' in *Unequal Achievement, The Irish Experience 1957-1982* Dublin, 1985.
24 Browne, Noel *Against the Tide* Dublin 1986 p. 158.
25 Ibid. pp. 158-159.
26 Caitríona Clear *Nuns in Nineteenth-Century Ireland* Dublin: 1987
27 *See* Nell McCafferty's *A Woman to Blame: The Kerry Babies Case* Dublin: Attic Press 1985
28 This refers to the piece of US legislation governing restriction on immigrants.
29 Irish Feminist Information was set up in 1978 and published the annual Irish Woman's Guidebook and Diary. In 1984, after successfully running two Women and Publishing training courses, IFI started the publishing imprint Attic press, now an independent company.
30 *See* Mary Lennon, Marie McAdam et al. *Across the Water* London 1988.

Select Bibliography

Arensberg, Conrad M and Kimball, Solon T *Family and Community in Ireland* Cambridge, 1968.

Bleakley, David *Sadie Patterson: Irish Peacemaker* Belfast, 1980.

Brown, Terence *Ireland: A Social and Cultural History 1922-1979* Glasgow, 1981.

Browne, Noel *Against the Tide* Dublin, 1986.

Clear, Caitríona *Nuns in Nineteenth-Century Ireland* Dublin, 1987.

Daly, Mary E *Dublin, The Deposed Capital: A Social and Economic History, 1860-1914* Cork, 1984.

Davis, Angela *Women, Race and Class* New York, 1981.

Drudy, PJ (ed) *The Irish in America: Emigration, Assimilation and Impact* Irish Studies 4 New York, 1985.

Dinar, Hasia R *Erin's Daughters in America: Irish Immigrant Women in the Nineteenth Century* Baltimore, Maryland, 1983.

Ewens, Elizabeth *Immigrant Women in the Land of Dollars: Life and Culture on the Lower East Side, 1890-1925* New York, 1985.

Fitzpatrick, D *Irish Emigration 1801-1921: Studies in Irish Economic and Social History 1* Dublin, 1984.

Gilligan, Carol *In a Different Voice: Psychological Theory and Women's Development* Cambridge, Mass, 1982.

Gurley Flynn, Elizabeth *Rebel Girl: An Autobiography, My First Life* New York, 1973.

Gurley Flynn, Elizabeth *Words on Fire: The Life and Writings of Elizabeth Gurley Flynn* New Brunswick, 1987.

Handlin, Oscar *Boston's Immigrants* Cambridge, Mass, 1941.

Handlin, Oscar *The Uprooted* New York, 1951.

Jones, Mother *Speeches and Writings of Mother Jones* Pittsburgh, Pa, 1988.

Kelly, Kate and Nic Giolla Choille, Triona *Emigration Matters for Women* Attic Press: Dublin, 1990.

Kennedy, Robert E *The Irish: Emigration, Marriage, and Fertility* Berkeley, 1973.

Kessler-Harris, Alice *Out to Work: A History of Wage-Earning Women in the United States* New York, 1982.

Lamphere, Louise *From Working Daughters to Working Mothers: Immigrant Women in a New England Industrial Community* Ithaca, New York, 1987.

Lee, JJ (ed) *Ireland 1945-1970* Dublin, 1979.

Lee, Joseph *The Modernisation of Irish Society 1848-1918* Dublin, 1973.

Lees, Lynn H *Exiles of Erin: Irish Migrants in Victorian London* New York, 1979.

Levenson, Leah and Natterstad, Jerry H *Hanna Sheehy-Skeffington: Irish Feminist.* Syracuse, 1986.

Lennon, Mary; McAdam, Marie and O'Brien, Joanne *Across the Water: Irish Women's Lives in Britain* London, 1988.

Lerner, Gerda *The Creation of Patriarchy* New York, 1986.

Loewenberg, Peter *Decoding the Past: the Psychohistorical Approach* Berkeley, 1985.

Lyons, FSL *Ireland Since the Famine* New York, 1971.

McCafferty, Nell *A Woman to Blame* Attic Press: Dublin, 1985.

MacCurtain, Margaret and O'Corrain, Donncha *Women in Irish Society: The Historical Dimension* Dublin, 1978.

Miller, Kirby A *Emigrants and Exiles: Ireland and the Irish Exodus to North America* New York, 1985.

Morrissey, Hazel *Betty Sinclair: A Woman's Fight for Socialism* Belfast, 1983.

Murphy, John A *Ireland in the Twentieth Century* Dublin, 1975.

Owens, Rosemary Cullen *Smashing Times: A History of the Irish Women's Suffrage Movement 1889-1922* Attic Press: Dublin 1984.

Rosaldo, Michelle Zimbalist and Lamphere, Louise *Woman Culture and Society* California, 1973.

Rowbotham, Sheila *Hidden From History: Three Hundred Years of Women's Oppression and the Fight Against it* London, 1973.

Scheper-Hughes, Nancy *Saints, Scholars, and Schizophrenics: Mental Illness in Rural Ireland* Berkeley, 1979.

Smyth, Ailbhe (ed) *Feminism in Ireland* Special Issue *Women's Studies International Forum* Vol 11 No 4. (Mail Order: Attic Press: Dublin).

Ward, Margaret *Unmanageable Revolutionaries: Women and Irish Nationalism* Dingle, Co Kerry, 1983.

Whyte, John *The Church and State in Modern Ireland 1923-1979* Dublin, 1974.

Journals/Articles/Papers

Boland, Eavan 'The Emigrant Irish' *The Massachusetts Review* Autumn, 1987.

Conroy, Róisín 'Images of Irish Women' *The Crane Bag*, Vol 4 No 1, 1980.

Drudy, PJ 'Irish Population Change and Emigration Since Independence' *The Irish in America: Emigration, Assimilation and Impact. Irish Studies 4*. Drudy, PJ (ed) New York, 1985.

Fitzpatrick, David 'A Share of the Honeycomb: Education, Emigration and Women.' Copy of work in progress, received from Professor Ruth-Ann Harris (Northeastern University, Boston) - no date indicated. Trinity College, Dublin.

Halpin, Bridie *Halpin Papers* c/o Christy Halpin, Long Island.

Jackson, Pauline 'Women in Nineteenth Century Irish Emigration.' *International Migration Review*, Vol 18, Winter 1984.

O'Carroll, Ide *O'Carroll Collection* Murray Research Centre on Women, Radcliffe College, Cambridge, Mass.

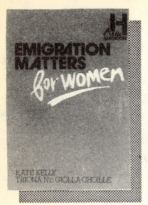

Emigration Matters for Women

Kate Kelly and Triona Nic Giolla Choille

"An important and valuable resource" *Irish Press*

Emigration Matters for Women is the only comprehensive handbook directly aimed at women thinking about emigrating and those who have already done so.

Offering far more than the usual directory, **Emigration Matters for Women** provides practical information and advice in the extensive and thorough resource section and compares different countries and what they have to offer women specifically. The authors clearly describe the decision-making process involved in emigration, the likely effects on the individual and the implications, both short and long-term, of leaving Ireland.

Uniquely, **Kate Kelly** and **Triona Nic Giolla Choille** place women's emigration now in the context of the history and experience of women's emigration over the past 150 years - a story largely untold until now.

Emigration Matters is for anyone dealing with the reality of emigration - parents, educators, community and youth workers - as well as for women emigrants and those considering emigration.

Kate Kelly and **Triona Nic Giolla Choille** are full-time information and education officers at the Emigrant Advice Centre in Dublin.

£4.95 / $9.95
96pp ISBN 0 946211 97 3

OTHER ATTIC TITLES OF INTEREST

Rosemary Cullen Owens
Smashing Times: A History of the Irish Women's Suffrage Movement 1889-1922 1984 160pp
ISBN 1 946211 078 £10.00 (hb) / 1 946211 086 £4.95 / $9.95 (pb)
"... urgently needs to be read by anyone interested in the foundations of modern Irish society." *Sunday Press*

Rosemary Cullen Owens
Did Your Granny Have a Hammer??? A History of Irish Women's Suffrage Movement 1985 140pp
£3.95 / $7.95 (Teaching pack)

Therese Caherty et al
More Missing Pieces: Her Story of Irish Women 1985 64pp
ISBN 1 946211 175 £2.95 / $5.95 (pb)

Ailbhe Smyth (ed)
Wildish Things: An Anthology of New Irish Women's Writing 1989 256pp
ISBN 1 946211 744 £15.95 (hb) / 1 946211 736 £7.95 / $15.95 (pb)
"Proof that we who read are in the midst of a revolution of the imagination." *The Irish Times*

Selected LIP Pamphlets
"Polemical pamphlets from women's lip ... It's more LIP we want, indeed." *The Irish Times*
Eavan Boland **A Kind of Scar: The Woman Poet in a National Tradition**
Edna Longley **From Cathleen to Anorexia - The Breakdown of Irelands**
Carol Coulter **Ireland - Between the First and the Third Worlds**

...and many more!

For catalogue, please contact **ATTIC PRESS** at
44 East Essex Street, Dublin 2.
Telephone (01) 716367 Fax (01) 6793754